UP IN A BALLOON

UP
IN
A
BALLOON

Leonard Cottrell

WORLD'S WORK LTD

BOOKS BY LEONARD COTTRELL

All men are neighbours
The Lost Pharaohs
Madame Tussaud
The Bull of Minos
Life under the Pharaohs
The Mountains of Pharaoh
One Man's Journey
Wonders of the World
Wonders of Antiquity
Land of the Two Rivers
Land of the Pharaohs
Seeing Roman Britain
The Great Invasion
Hannibal, Enemy of Rome
Crete, Island of Mystery
Digs and Diggers
Lost Cities
Lost Worlds
Encyclopaedia of Archaeology (Ed.)
The Tiger of Ch'in
The Land of Shinar
The Anvil of Civilisation
A Guide to Egypt
The Lion Gate
Realms of Gold
Lady of the Two Lands
Five Queens of Ancient Egypt
"Archaeology" in "The Great Ideas Today"
The Warrior Pharaohs

Copyright © 1970 by S. G. Phillips, Inc.
First published in Great Britain 1974 by
World's Work Ltd
The Windmill Press
Kingswood, Tadworth, Surrey
Printed by offset in Great Britain by
William Clowes & Sons, Limited
London, Beccles and Colchester
SBN 437 32850 3

To

Marjorie Drakeford

in friendship

When he bestrides the lazy-pacing clouds
And sails upon the bosom of the air.

—SHAKESPEARE

Acknowledgments

I wish to acknowledge the help I have derived from the following sources (those marked with an asterisk have been quoted):

* *The Andrée Diaries* (John Lane The Bodley Head, London, 1931)

  H. Coxwell, *My Life and Balloon Experiences* (W. H. Allen, London, 1887)

* W. de Fonvielle, *Adventures in the Air* (Edward Standford, London, 1877)

* C. H. Gibbs-Smith, *A History of Flying* (Batsford, London, 1953)

* James Glaisher, with Flammarion, de Fonvielle, and Tissandier, *Travels in the Air* (Richard Bentley, London, 1871)

* F. Stansbury Haydon, *Aeronautics in the Union and Confederate Armies* (Johns Hopkins Press, Baltimore, 1941)

* A. Hildebrandt, *Airships Past and Present* (Constable, London, 1908)
* V. Lunardi, *Account of the First Aerial Voyage in England* (London, 1784)
* Monck Mason, *Aeronautica* (Westley, London, 1848)
* L. T. C. Rolt, *The Aeronauts* (Longmans, London, 1966)
  Alberto Santos-Dumont, *My Airships* (Grant Richards, London, 1904)
  E. Seton Valentine and F. L. Tomlinson, *Travels in Space* (Hurst & Blackett, London, 1912)

I also wish to acknowledge the help I have received from the staffs of the London Library, the B.B.C. Library, and the Royal Aeronautical Society of London.

July 1969   LEONARD COTTRELL

Contents

List of Illustrations

ACKNOWLEDGMENTS

The illustrations on pages 109 and 154 are used by courtesy of the Smithsonian Institution, Washington, D.C. The illustrations on pages 83 and 146 are reproduced by courtesy of the Rare Book Division, The New York Public Library. The photograph on page 184 is used by permission of Svenska Sällskapet for Antropologi och Geografi, Sweden. The illustration on page 16 is Crown Copyright and is reproduced by permission of the Science Museum, London. The other photographs and engravings are reproduced by kind permission of C. H. Gibbs-Smith Esq.

Introduction

This book is not meant to be a complete history of ballooning but rather an account of man's first successful attempts to free himself of the earth and realize the dream of flying which has obsessed him from very early times. I have confined myself to the free balloon, ignoring both the airship and the aeroplane, because in these days of supersonic aircraft and spacecraft one tends to forget the courage, daring, and enterprise of those early aeronauts. Trusting only to a frail, gas-filled envelope, they ventured into regions which men had never entered before and which were as full of unknown hazards as outer space is today.

Some of the stories of these early aeronauts are heroic, some tragic, some humorous, because the man-carrying balloon, since it was first invented nearly two centuries ago, has been put to many uses, both serious and frivolous. In the late eighteenth century it was the fashionable fad of the French aristocrats to whom it was first demonstrated. Soon it developed into a form of mass entertainment, and crowds flocked to watch balloon ascents from the pleasure grounds of Europe and the United States. Some of the more daring even made ascents themselves under the care of professional "balloon pilots," who became popular heroes, like the astronauts of today.

But there was another side of ballooning, or "aerostatics," as it used to be called. Men of science realized its value in exploring the upper atmosphere and, either alone or assisted by professional aeronauts, made daring ascents into the unknown regions of the upper air.

Women also played a part in the development of ballooning, and it may surprise many to know that as early as 1804 some of them were making solo ascents. At least one girl became a professional parachutist, giving many demonstrations.

Not surprisingly, there were many accidents, some fatal, yet the intrepid aeronauts continued to brave the air in their frail craft, either to make money by entertaining the crowd or to gratify their lust for adventure or in the interests of science. Other aspects of ballooning to which I have given some attention are the use of balloons in warfare and in exploration.

Throughout this book I have concentrated attention on the personalities and often incredible achievements of the balloonists rather than on the technicalities of ballooning itself.

Chapter 1

The first men
to fly

For many thousands of years man has dreamed of being able to fly. This dream is expressed in the legends of many countries—such as those of Daedalus, who made wings to escape from Crete with his son Icarus, of Sinbad, who was carried aloft on the back of a giant bird, and of the flying carpet of Oriental folktales. Quite apart from legend, man has at various times tried to imitate the birds and has actually made himself wings, which did not work. And as long ago as the fifteenth century Leonardo da Vinci designed flying machines, the drawings of which still exist. He even made a model helicopter, driven by clockwork, which flew.

Nowadays we are so accustomed to powered flight that we tend to forget that it was in balloons that men began to make aerial journeys, nearly two hundred years ago. It is not easy to take the balloon seriously. There is something absurd about its very appearance. Unwieldy, fat, and apparently helpless, it is associated with the toys of children. Yet it was man-carrying balloons which first conquered the air; they covered huge distances and attained enormous heights, and the art of handling them bred generations of brave and skilful

15

Early design for an Aerial Ship, by Francesco de Lana, 1670, using evacuated spheres

airmen long before the first powered aircraft lumbered off the ground at Kitty Hawk in 1903.

It is important to remember, too, that the early aeronauts ventured into an environment which was as unfamiliar to them as outer space is to us. They knew very little about the blanket of air which thinly covers the earth's surface. They knew almost nothing about air currents or about hot and cold fronts, and they had no weather forecasts to guide them on their perilous and lonely journeys. Even the powerful aircraft of today need these guides to safe navigation, although even the most lightly powered aircraft is less vulnerable to the elements than the balloon, which cannot be steered.

Nevertheless, it would be quite wrong to assume that little skill was needed in balloon navigation. The balloonist had two means of control. If he found himself being forced earthward by downward currents, he could gain extra lift by throwing out ballast. If he found himself rising too high, into regions where breathing became difficult, he could open a valve, thus releasing gas from the balloon, and lose height. The same principle applied when he wished to land. Using only these two means of control, the balloon pilot could, if he was both skilful and lucky, take off, level out at what he considered a suitable height, rise to clear hills and mountains, and descend when he saw a suitable landing place. What he could not do was to change course.

In time balloonists learned something about cloud formations and the type of air currents they might encounter near or within them. They could then sometimes choose their line of flight by ascending or descending when they thought that the wind would bear them in a certain direction. Even so, the pioneers had no means of knowing if the wind was likely to change in force or direction, or whether, having reached a certain height, they might encounter air currents which would endanger their craft or carry them off their intended course. There was always an element of hazard in ballooning, and this attracted intrepid men of many nationalities. It still does, and ballooning remains a popular sport for a few dedicated enthusiasts.

There are two ways of making a balloon rise. One way is to fill it with hot air, a continuous supply of which has to be maintained, of course, while the balloon is in flight. This means carrying aloft a furnace to heat the air, with all the attendant danger of setting fire to the fabric. The other way is to fill the envelope with a gas which is lighter than air, such as hydrogen. Hydrogen is highly inflammable, and one spark, or a lightning flash, would be sufficient to ignite the gas and destroy the balloon. Today there are lighter-than-air gases, such as helium, which are not inflammable, but in the eighteenth century such gases were unknown, and only hydrogen was available.

The principle of hot air expanding and rising seems so obvious to us that we may wonder why mankind had to wait until 1783 for someone to think of filling a bag with the stuff and sending it aloft. No elaborate technical apparatus is necessary. The highly intelligent ancient Greeks could have done it, just as one of them, Hiero of Alexandria, invented a primitive form of steam engine. Yet how many generations had watched steam issuing from a kettle before James Watt realized that the force which raised the kettle lid could be harnessed to drive machinery? It seems that great inventions such as this can take place only in an age when the climate of opinion favours them.

The eighteenth century was such an age. Although the European masses remained relatively uneducated and illiterate, and even the educated minority were usually conventional, credulous, and superstitious, there were some men who, following the example of such great scientists as Newton, Boyle, and Locke, had trained their minds to inquire deeply into the laws of nature. They were not content to accept unthinkingly what most people took for granted. They did not merely observe that such and such a thing happened, as, for example, a lightning flash. They wanted to know *why* it happened and if there was any system of natural laws which *made* it happen. One example of such men was the great American Benjamin Franklin, who flew a kite in a storm, attached a door key to the lower end of the string, and saw a spark fly off the key, proving that what the storm clouds were releasing was stored-up electricity.

One scientific inquirer of the eighteenth century, a man who experimented and questioned, was Joseph Montgolfier, whose father was the well-to-do owner of a paper factory at Annonay in France. Joseph was born in 1740 and died in 1810; his younger brother, Jacques Etienne, was born in 1745 and died in 1799, As with other distinguished men, a number of legends have sprung up around them, one of which says that Joseph noticed—as millions had done before him—that clouds formed by smoke are not unlike some clouds formed by water vapour. Smoke rises, and clouds remain suspended in the atmosphere. Therefore, Joseph asked himself, "If I were to fill a container with smoke, would it not also rise?" Another story tells how Joseph, while staying at an inn at Avignon, saw a shirt, which had been put to air in front of the fire, suddenly take off and rise as hot air filled it. This and similar stories remind one of the tale of Watt and the steaming kettle. There may be some truth in them.

It is certain that Joseph Montgolfier was keenly interested in the scientific discoveries of his time, particularly in physics. He had read a translation of a paper written by a British scientist, Joseph Priestley, called "Experiments and Observations in Different Kinds of Airs," and he was no doubt aware that in 1766 another

British scientist, Henry Cavendish, had succeeded in making hydrogen, which he called "inflammable air," by the action of sulphuric acid on iron.

Certainly in the year 1782 Joseph's mind was already considering the possibility of making man-carrying balloons. At this time France, allied to Spain, was at war with Britain, and their combined armies and navies were trying to take Gibraltar. Joseph wrote to the military authorities: "I possess a superhuman means of introducing our soldiers into this impregnable fortress. . . . They may enter through the air; the gas produced by the combustion of a little straw or a few rags should not pass, like the subtle inflammable air [hydrogen] through the pores of a paper bag. By making a bag large enough, it will be possible to introduce into Gibraltar an entire army, which, borne by the wind, will enter right above the heads of the English."

Thus, nearly two centuries ago, Joseph Montgolfier anticipated the idea of airborne troops.

The reference to the "subtle inflammable air" suggests that at this time Montgolfier had abandoned the idea of using hydrogen because he had not devised an envelope of a material dense enough to contain it. (Also it was difficult to produce hydrogen in quantity.) He concentrated instead on the "gas" which he believed was produced in smoke, particularly the smoke of burning wool and straw. He made experiments, together with his younger brother (some say in the kitchen of their home at Annonay), and was delighted when paper bags filled with smoke rose to the ceiling.

Greatly encouraged, the brothers transferred their activities to the open air—perhaps their cook objected to seeing her kitchen filled with floating objects. In a field near Lyon they lit a bonfire, filled a much larger bag with smoke, and set it free. Before the eyes of the bewildered spectators the bag rose to a height of a thousand feet before falling to the ground.

They had started from the mistaken belief that the smoke caused the balloon to rise, whereas the smoke had nothing to do with it. It was the heated air which, expanding within the bag and becoming lighter than the surrounding atmosphere, forced the bag to ascend. Later the Montgolfiers realized this and improved on their performance. They made larger and larger balloons, using silk, and on June 5th, 1783, one of these rose to a height estimated at six thousand feet, landing one and a half miles from its starting point. From this time onward, hot-air balloons were called *montgolfières*.

However, the honour of sending up the first balloon from the capital, Paris, fell to Professor Jacques Alexandre César Charles, a scientist of great repute, who for years had been producing hydrogen in his laboratory. He was a firm believer in the hydrogen balloon and had discovered that an envelope made of goldbeater's skin (a prepared animal membrane used to separate the leaves of gold foil during the process of beating) would, if reinforced with a sheet of rubber, be sufficiently dense to contain the hydrogen. Before the brothers from Annonay arrived in Paris, Professor Charles' balloon was ready.

The filling of the envelope with hydrogen presented no great difficulties. The balloon was fixed to a cask containing the sulphuric acid and iron filings which produced the hydrogen. There were holes in the top of the cask, one leading to the interior of the balloon, and another open to receive the acid and the iron. But

21

Charles made one mistake. He incorporated in the base of his balloon a pipe with a tap. By closing this tap, of which he was very proud, Charles believed that he would prevent wastage of gas and allow his craft to ascend higher and stay aloft longer.

Every scientific precaution was taken to ensure that there would be no accidents. For example, at first the balloon was allowed to rise while anchored to a rope which prevented it from ascending above a certain height. But when the Parisians saw this strange, beautiful sphere, resplendent in its bright colours, ascend high above their roofs, they flocked to the vicinity of the Place des Victoires, where the experiments were being made, and tried to storm the enclosure. Professor Charles decided to move his balloon to the more spacious environment of the Champ-de-Mars (where the Eiffel Tower now stands). The hydrogen-filled sphere, aloft above its cart, was taken, under armed guard, through the streets of Paris at night by the light of torches. If one spark had touched the balloon, it would have burst into flames, but Charles was lucky, and no accident occurred.

The date was August 27th, 1783. At five in the afternoon a cannon boomed, and the balloon, called the *Globe*, rose swiftly and majestically in a fierce shower of rain. Thousands of spectators watched it, entranced, unheeding the downpour. They saw something which no Parisian had ever seen before, a man-made object soaring high into the dark clouds, which temporarily hid it from view. After a time it reappeared at a higher altitude, a mere speck in the sky, and again the cannon boomed. Then the balloon was lost again, and it was not until the next day that news reached Paris that it had descended to earth in a field at Genoesse, about fifteen miles away, where terrified and superstitious peasants had attacked it with pitchforks.

Among the crowd who watched Charles' balloon on that day was Benjamin Franklin. It is said that a by-stander turned to him as the balloon was lost to view and remarked with a grin, "And of what use is it?" Franklin thought for a moment and then replied, "Of what use is a newborn baby?"

The reason for the balloon's descent after such a short journey became apparent when Charles examined the remains of the envelope. A rent in one of the seams, not caused by the infuriated peasants, proved that it had burst. And the cause was the closed tap at its base. What Charles had not realized was that, as the balloon rose higher into the more rarefied atmosphere, the pressure on its outer skin grew less while the pressure of the gas inside remained the same. So it blew up. There was no means, as in the montgolfières, of allowing the gas to escape and so equalizing the pressure.

Professor Charles' experiment had been highly successful, but nonetheless the balloon had not carried any freight—not even a few animals, let alone a man. The Montgolfier brothers decided, when King Louis XVI agreed that they should give a demonstration at his palace at Versailles, to improve on Charles' experiment. Their balloon, of the hot-air type, had a basket suspended beneath it containing a cock, a sheep, and a duck. The basic idea was scientific: to discover whether or not living creatures could survive the aerial journey. If they could, then men could surely follow.

So, three weeks after Charles' hydrogen balloon had made its flight, a great crowd gathered at Versailles. The

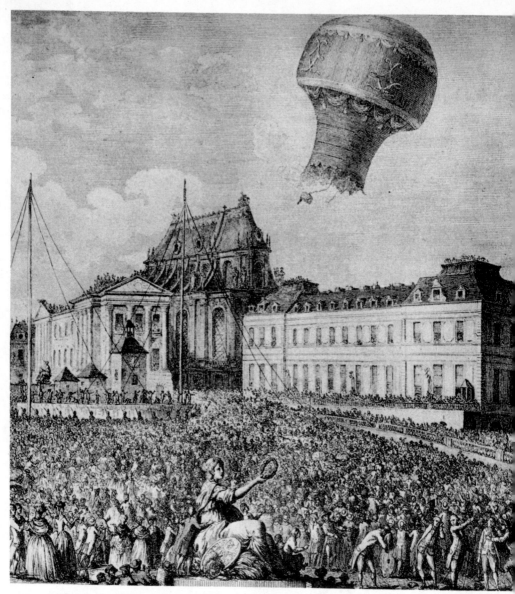

The "animal ascent" in which a sheep, cock and duck ascended beneath a
Montgolfier hot-air balloon from Versailles, September 19th, 1783

King and members of the court, seated in the Cours des
Ministres, saw the Montgolfiers' assistants struggling to
hold the balloon against the wind, while others stoked
up the fire to produce the hot air needed to inflate it.
This was far removed from that moment when, in a field

near Lyon, the brothers had lit bonfires to make smoke to fill a large paper bag. This time the King of France was watching, and they were surrounded by distinguished men of science. So many things could go wrong. The silken envelope might catch fire, or it might get out of control once it began to inflate, or it might spring a leak. And the Montgolfiers knew that among the scores of thousands watching them on that day, there were many who hoped they would fail, for some people regarded the balloon as the invention of devils.

Gradually the fabric began to fill with hot air. It bulged and swayed in the wind. The assistants hung on to the ropes to keep it under control, and the crowd roared with excitement. After a long time it distended into a sphere and rose a few feet from the ground, while the assistants strained to prevent it from rising prematurely. They then had to attach the basket carrying the duck, the rooster, and the sheep.

This accomplished, the signal was given to let go the ropes; and, to the exultant cries of the crowd, the multi-coloured globe, carrying its animal freight, rose into the air and in an astonishingly short time soared high above Versailles until it appeared only the size of a tennis ball, carried swifty by the wind. The brothers Montgolfier knew, of course, that it could not maintain its flight for very long. As soon as the hot air cooled, the balloon would begin to deflate and would have to descend. They, and many others, set off in pursuit, on horseback. The King and his court, highly impressed, returned to the palace to discuss this "miracle."

The first balloon to carry living creatures came to earth safely in the wood of Vaucresson, having gone a distance of only two miles. But during that journey it had reached 1,500 feet, as was ascertained by two astronomers, Jeaurat and Le Gentil, using the triangulation method. The animals survived unscathed, apart from the cock, which had a broken wing. This, however, was not due to its rough landing, but to having been violently kicked by the sheep just before takeoff.

To introduce the next participant in this story, we have to return to the moment when Professor Charles' burst hydrogen balloon descended in a field near Genoesse. The first man to arrive on the scene, after the angry peasants, was a young scholar, historian, and scientist named Jean-François Pilâtre de Rozier. He had ridden after the balloon from Paris; and when, having arrived on the scene, he saw Joseph Montgolfier approaching, he embraced him with the words "*I* was the first to arrive!" The two became friends, and later, when it was proposed to construct a montgolfière to carry human passengers, Pilâtre de Rozier persuaded the Montgolfiers to let him be the first man to fly. (Thus the historian would write himself into history. Curiously, the Montgolfier brothers themselves showed no great eagerness to take to the air.)

The new balloon was constructed in Paris under the direction of Joseph Montgolfier and was inflated in the garden of a paper-maker named Reveillon. It was forty-six feet wide and sixty-six feet high, with a circular gallery beneath, attached by a multiple of cords and surrounded by a balustrade three and a half feet high to keep the aeronaut from falling overboard if he turned giddy when he found himself high above the earth. Above the gallery, and below the hole at the bottom of the balloon, was a pan on which straw and wool could be burned to maintain the continuous supply of hot air

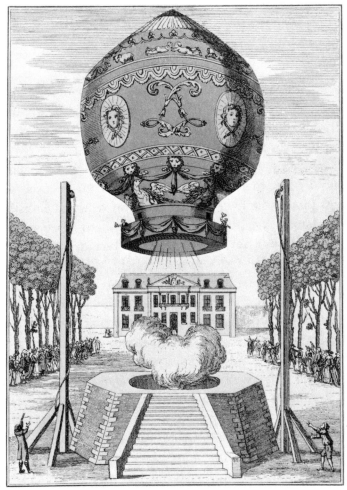

The first aerial voyage in history by Pilâtre de Rozier and the
Marquis D'Arlandes in a Montgolfier hot-air balloon,
November 21st, 1783, over Paris

which would enable the balloon to make longer journeys.
The aeronaut would be responsible for keeping the fire
going, using fuel stored in the gallery.

When the balloon was first tested at the end of a
rope, young Pilâtre de Rozier revealed himself as a natural pilot. On October 15th, 1783, he made his first
ascent—to a height of eighty feet. Soon he discovered
that, by adjusting the amount of rags and straw (moist-
ened with alcohol) that he fed to the flames, he could
make the balloon ascend or descend at will. Sometimes

he would suddenly arrest his descent; sometimes he would allow himself to be carried rapidly to the ground. All he had to do was to throw a few handfuls of straw into the pan to effect a new ascent.

In short, Monsieur Pilâtre de Rozier was enjoying himself. But then came a serious hitch in the proceedings. Just as the intrepid aeronaut was ready to make his untethered ascent into the atmosphere, Louis XVI stepped in and forbade it. After all, was not Pilâtre de Rozier a scholar and a state historian? Why should such a precious life be hazarded when there were numerous condemned criminals in the Paris prisons who could be sent up instead? King Louis suggested that, if one or two condemned felons were sent up in the montgolfière, and survived, they could be pardoned and set free, whereas otherwise they were bound to lose their heads anyway. It seemed at first an eminently practical suggestion, but it shocked and outraged Pilâtre de Rozier.

The would-be pilot wrote indignantly that *les viles criminels* should not be allowed the honour of being the first men on earth to fly. It was no use; Louis XVI remained adamant. But Pilâtre de Rozier did not despair. He happened to know the Duchesse de Polignac, who was on intimate terms with the Queen, Marie Antoinette. He persuaded the Duchess to intercede with the Queen on his behalf, and eventually the Queen induced the King to withdraw his order and give Pilâtre de Rozier permission to fly. So two women (at least) were indirectly responsible for the first attempt by man to bring to reality Shakespeare's poetic dream:

When he bestrides the lazy-pacing clouds
And sails upon the bosom of the air.

The date of the ascent was fixed as November 21st, 1783. In the meantime, a young aristocrat, the Marquis d'Arlandes, persuaded Pilâtre de Rozier to let him go along on this historic adventure. It is to d'Arlandes, and not to Pilâtre de Rozier, that we owe the firsthand account of man's first successful attempt to fly. Considering that for thousands of years men had dreamed of flying and that this was to be the first time the dream was realized, one would expect a much more dramatic and poetic story; but in fact d'Arlandes' account is quite ordinary, almost commonplace, except for flashes of humour. It is in the form of a dialogue between Pilâtre de Rozier and himself, and to appreciate it one must understand that the two aeronauts, stationed at opposite ends of the gallery, could not see each other, the huge neck of the balloon coming between them. They therefore had to shout their messages. Apparently it was d'Arlandes' task to refuel the fire under the balloon while Pilâtre de Rozier navigated; but the young Marquis was so entranced by the view that he tended to forget his duties.

The launching place was at the Château de la Muette, in the Bois de Boulogne, and at 2:00 p.m. the *Globe*, as this balloon also was named, rose into the sky, carrying with it the first human beings to embark on an aerial voyage. The craft (or *aerostat*, as such balloons were called) passed over Paris at a fairly low altitude, and from every street, window, and rooftop scores of thousands of Parisians watched its passage, some shouting with delight and approval, some stunned into silence, some weeping with emotion.

High above their spectators, the aeronauts experienced at first a feeling of extraordinary calm and peace.

They had no sense of movement; rather it seemed that the earth was moving below them while they remained stationary. Here is some of the dialogue which the Marquis d'Arlandes later wrote down:

Pilâtre de Rozier: "You are doing nothing! The balloon is rising scarcely a fathom!"

D'Arlandes (throwing some straw upon the fire): "Pardon!"

D'Arlandes then went on to say that he turned quickly, "but already we had passed out of sight of La Muette. Astonished, I cast a glance towards the river. I perceived the confluence of the Oise, and naming the principal bends of the river by the places nearest them I cried, 'Passy, St. Germain, St. Denis, Sèvres!' "

Pilâtre de Rozier: "If you look at the river in that fashion you will be likely to bathe in it soon. Some fire, my dear friend, some fire!"

Obediently the Marquis added more fuel to the pan, and the balloon began to gain a little height. The narrative continues: "We travelled on; but instead of crossing the river, as our direction seemed to indicate, we bore towards the Invalides, then returned upon the principal bed of the river, dodging about it but not crossing it."

D'Arlandes: "This river is very difficult to cross!"

Pilâtre de Rozier: "So it seems, but you are doing nothing. I suppose it is because you are braver than I and do not fear to fall!"

Stung by this remark, d'Arlandes picked up a truss of straw with a fork and heaped it on the flames. Immediately he felt himself "lifted as it were to the Heavens."

D'Arlandes: "At last we move!"

Pilâtre de Rozier: "Yes, we move."

Shortly after this d'Arlandes reported that he "heard

from the top of the balloon a sound which made me believe it had burst. I watched, yet I saw nothing. . . . As my eyes were fixed on the top of the machine I experienced a shock, and it was the only one I had felt." The movement of the balloon suddenly became agitated, and Pilâtre de Rozier called out to his unseen companion.

Pilâtre de Rozier: "What are you doing? Having a dance by yourself?"

D'Arlandes: "I have not moved."

Pilâtre de Rozier: "So much the better. It is only a new current. It may carry us from the river."

D'Arlandes: "We are getting on."

Pilâtre de Rozier: "Let us work! Let us work!"

More fuel was fed to the flames, which leaped higher. D'Arlandes then heard another cracking sound, which he thought must be due to the parting of a cord. He looked inside the envelope and noticed that the part which was turned towards the south had been burned full of holes of considerable size. He called out to his companion.

D'Arlandes: "It must descend!"

Pilâtre de Rozier: "Why?"

D'Arlandes: "Look and see for yourself!"

The Marquis then "took a sponge and quietly extinguished the little fire that was burning some of the holes within my reach; but at the same time I noticed that the bottom of the cloth was coming away from the circle which surrounded it." He repeated to his companion: "We must descend."

Behind the stilted eighteenth-century dialogue one can sense the drama of that moment, and even glimpse the characters of the two men; both brave, but Pilâtre de Rozier perhaps a little calmer than his companion.

D'Arlandes' story continues: "I examined from my side and saw that we had nothing to fear. I then tried, with my sponge, the ropes which were within my reach. All of them held firm. I then said: 'We can cross Paris.'"

But could they? By this time they were almost down to rooftop level. D'Arlandes threw more straw onto the fire, and smoke billowed up into the balloon, which began to quickly rise again. "I looked down," wrote the Marquis, "and it seemed to me we were going towards the towers of St. Sulpice; but on rising, a new current made us quit this direction and bear more to the south. I looked to the left and saw a wood, which I believed to be that of Luxembourg. I cried all at once: 'Get to the ground.'"

D'Arlandes must have been a singularly honest man, for at this stage of the flight he clearly panicked. But he went on to praise Pilâtre de Rozier: "But the intrepid Rozier, who never lost his head, and who judged more surely than I, prevented me from attempting to descend. I threw a bundle of straw on the fire. We rose again, and another current bore us to the left. We were now close to the ground, between two mills. As soon as we came near the earth, I raised myself over the gallery, and, leaning there with my two hands, I felt the balloon pressing softly against my head. I pushed it back and leaped to the ground. Looking round and expecting to see the balloon still distended, I was astonished to find it quite empty, and flattened. On looking for de Rozier, I saw him in his shirtsleeves creeping out from under the mass of fabric that had fallen on him."

It was only twenty-five minutes since the aeronauts had left the Château de la Muette. They had landed a little over five miles from where they started. But the distance was unimportant. Charles' hydrogen balloon had flown higher and traveled farther, but it was the clumsy hot-air montgolfière which first carried men on an aerial journey.

Professor Charles, firm believer in the hydrogen balloon, was not long in seeking to prove the superiority of his type of aerostat. He obtained permission to make an ascent from the Tuileries gardens in Paris, and to prove his faith in his invention he proposed to make the ascent himself. The King, having granted permission for Pilâtre de Rozier and d'Arlandes to fly in the montgolfière, could hardly refuse to permit Professor Charles to make a similar flight.

Charles, accompanied by a young man named Robert, rose gracefully from the Tuileries gardens on December 1st, 1783, in a hydrogen-filled balloon only twenty-seven feet in diameter (against the Montgolfiers' forty-six feet). The balloon ascended rapidly to a height of 1,880 feet, as registered by the barometer which the aeronauts carried with them. Eventually they came to earth at the village of Nesles, twenty-seven miles away, having been aloft for one and three-quarter hours, more than four times as long as the duration of their rivals' voyage. But, if there was rivalry between the Montgolfiers and Charles, it was friendly: Charles, who had invited Joseph Montgolfier to watch the ascent, gave him the honour of cutting the cord which released the balloon—a delicate compliment to the man who had devised the first craft which carried men into the air.

Neither Professor Charles nor his companion seemed any worse for their adventure, which they described as having been calm and pleasant. In fact, the professor was so exultant that shortly after landing he decided to make

The inflation of a hydrogen balloon with gas made from sulphuric acid poured over iron filings. The balloon is suspended by the crown during the inflation

a second flight by himself. In his enthusiasm, however, he forgot that, relieved of the weight of his colleague, the balloon would rise much faster. It zoomed into the air at a furious speed and was soon lost to view, while poor Professor Charles, alone and hanging on to the rope which supported the basket, saw the earth at a height from which no human being, apart from mountaineers, had ever seen it before. Although this time he had left open the tap which allowed hydrogen to escape and so equalize the pressure, he must have been horribly alarmed lest the balloon should burst and send him hurtling to earth. He reached a height of more than nine thousand feet, and during the twenty-five minutes he was aloft the craft was flung violently this way and that by turbulent air currents. It was a wild ride, and the professor never again ventured into the air.

The first ascent in history by a hydrogen balloon December 1st, 1783 at Paris. The scene shown here is when, after J. C. Charles, the pilot, had dropped the elder of the Robert brothers at Nesle he went up again on his own

Chapter 2

Ballooning spreads

The success of Professor Charles and the Montgolfier brothers sparked off an explosion of activity in France which could be called balloon mania. Once it had been demonstrated that men could be carried aloft in balloons, hundreds wanted to share the experience, especially in Paris. And for people who had neither the ability nor the resources to make a full-sized aerostat, there remained miniature balloons which could be made or bought quite cheaply. They were usually of paper, gaily painted, with a small pan underneath in which a fire could be lit. Soon the air above Paris was full of these dangerous objects, floating over the rooftops by day and night, and sometimes starting fires when they descended. In fact, the danger became so great that a law had to be passed forbidding their use.

But there was no stopping the movement. The city of Lyon, near which the first experiments in "aerostation" had taken place, was determined not to be outdone by Paris. The Montgolfier brothers were induced to construct a very large hot-air balloon called the *Fleselles*. One hundred feet in diameter, about one hundred and thirty feet high, it was probably the largest balloon ever made. On January 19th, 1784, it made its stately ascent from Lyon with seven passengers: Pilâtre de Rozier (the hero of the hour), members of the local aristocracy (including the Comte de Laurencin, the Comte de Dampierre, and Prince Charles de Ligne), and none other than Joseph Montgolfier himself.

A huge fire, fed by trusses of straw, had to be kept alight below the balloon, and the sight of this great object underlit by the fiery glow must have been superb to the watchers on the ground, though less so to the occupants of the gondola which swung below the balloon. It lumbered into the air, and rose to 3,000 feet. After a quarter of an hour it had to descend because a split in the envelope allowed the hot air to escape. But the *Fleselles* did not catch fire, and no one was hurt when it landed. The occupants appeared triumphantly at the local theatre that night and received a tremendous ovation.

In June of the following year, 1785, another ascent was made from Lyon, graced by the presence in the gondola of the first-known female aeronaut, a Madame Thible, who is said to have been an extremely attractive woman. She was piloted by a Monsieur Fleurant and, on being carried aloft, burst into song with the words "Je triomphe, je suis reine" ("I triumph, I am queen") from the opera *La Belle Arsène*. Monsieur Fleurant sang in reply, "Quoi, voyager dans les nuages" ("Travel among the clouds"). That night the first female aeronaut received an enthusiastic welcome when she appeared on the stage of the theatre, "she was presented with a coronet of flowers amid the applause of the whole assembly."

Gustavus, King of Sweden, happened to be travelling through Lyon and saw this spectacle. It was arranged that an even more remarkable demonstration should be staged at Versailles on his behalf. A huge montgolfière, lavishly decorated with the intertwined symbols of Louis and Gustavus, was named the *Marie Antoinette*. The wind, however, was so strong at the time of its launching that only Pilâtre de Rozier (whom one admires more and more) and one other gentleman could be persuaded to enter the gondola. With the two monarchs and the court watching, the balloon finally rose. Even with the fierce fire maintained to keep the balloon aloft it sank to earth after less than three quarters of an hour. It set fire to a tree and then to itself, ending in an inferno of flame, from which Pilâtre de Rozier and his companion were lucky to escape alive.

This use of ballooning for entertainment distressed the scientists, especially the Montgolfier brothers, Professor Charles, and Pilâtre de Rozier. Why should their wonderful invention be reduced to the level of a mere theatrical display? Charles and the Montgolfiers were dedicated men of science, as was Pilâtre de Rozier, who had risked his life several times to prove the practicability of aerostatic flight. They became increasingly angry at the debasement of their invention. Joseph Montgolfier's imaginative idea of dropping balloon troops on Gibraltar was never taken seriously, though it might have worked, given the right conditions. Pilâtre de Rozier, though he had received a pension of 2,000 *livres* from the King, still hankered after something which would force his patrons to take the balloon seriously.

An idea struck him. Why not combine the montgolfière and the hydrogen balloons? The hydrogen-filled envelope would maintain the craft in the air at a good altitude. The montgolfière, attached to it below, would, by the addition or subtraction of an insignificant amount of burning fuel, enable it to ascend and descend rapidly at will, thus taking advantage of prevailing air currents. It was an inspired idea, and no one seems to have concerned himself with the fact that lighting an open fire below an envelope of highly inflammable gas was courting disaster.

Several combined balloons of this kind were constructed, and all ended unhappily, not because of a conflagration, but because the Paris mob, enraged by being kept waiting for hours for the hydrogen envelope to be inflated, stormed onto the launching field and ripped the balloons to pieces. It cannot be emphasized too strongly that the pioneer aeronauts were struggling not only against the frivolous and erratic patronage of the court and the aristocracy, but also against the blind, ignorant prejudice of the mob, whose attitude to balloonists combined fascination with superstitious terror. To the mass of the population they were little better than magicians, in league with the Devil; hence the fury with which the peasants of Genoesse destroyed Professor Charles' hydrogen balloon with their pitchforks.

From the very beginning, ballooning attracted showmen as well as men of science. These people saw in the balloon an opportunity to make money by exploiting the love of the dangerous and spectacular. One of these men was Jean-Pierre Blanchard. A self-educated showman, he had shown an uncommon aptitude for mechanics even from the age of sixteen, and is credited with the invention of the velocipede, the first wheeled vehicle which could be moved by human power—a relative of the bicycle.

Blanchard tried, without success, to make heavier-than-air flying machines, but when Professor Charles demonstrated the power and versatility of the hydrogen balloon, Blanchard realized that there was no immediate future for heavier-than-air craft.

Then he conceived the "controllable airship" with which he hoped to outdo both Charles and Montgolfier. It was to be equipped with large oars, which Blanchard, like other aeronauts after him, believed would enable him to control the motion of the balloon. He did not realize that air is so thin, compared with water, that only powered "oars"—mechanically propelled airscrews —could hope to make an impression on it. And in 1784 there was no motive power practical for aircraft except human muscles.

Blanchard constructed such a balloon. It was equipped with vast oars and a sort of frill round its middle which he called a parachute. It flew from the Champ-de-Mars on March 2nd, 1784. Just before takeoff a young cadet named Dupont, of the Military Academy at Brienne, tried to force his way into the gondola in place of the priest whom Blanchard had arranged to take with him. Prevented by the crowd, the young man drew his sword and slashed the balloon. It nevertheless took off as planned and, despite its oars, behaved just like any other balloon, though Blanchard refused to admit it.

Other people, such as Louis-Bernard Guyton de Morveau of the Academy of Dijon, experimented with so-called "controllable balloons," and the Robert brothers (one of whom had flown with Professor Charles) are stated to have "managed to navigate a curve nearly one kilometer in radius" in an airship flown in 1784 with a crew of six. They used large oars of silk stretched on frames. If this feat was accomplished, it must have been in absolutely still air. Eventually it had to be accepted that, lacking mechanical power, a control mechanism was unable to battle with the wind.

In other experiments, Guyton de Morveau tried coal gas as a lifting agent, but in the end returned to the method of producing hydrogen by the action of acetic acid on zinc. (Others used sulphuric acid and iron filings. Perhaps the most ingenious experiment was an attempt to fill a balloon from the gas produced by distilling potatoes; it failed.)

Many scientists of Europe took balloons very seriously, foreseeing both their military and their scientific possibilities. When the news of the great experiment by the Montgolfiers reached St. Petersburg, in Russia, in 1783, the great mathematician Leonard Euler, who was nearly eighty years old and blind, made mathematical calculations on a slate to determine the height to which a balloon could rise into the atmosphere. After he died, his eldest son sent the calculations to the Paris Academy of Sciences, which published them. But little notice was taken, and even in 1877, nearly a century after Euler made his calculations, Wildfrid de Fonvielle, author of *Adventures in the Air*, sadly commented that "the mathematical theory of the motion of balloons is still much as he [Euler] left it upon his slate." The great chemist Lavoisier was also keenly interested, and made a report "on the advantages which may be derived from the invention of balloons," and another scholar, the Abbé Bertholon, professor of physics at the Montpellier Academy, pointed out that balloons could be used effectively to carry emissaries and messengers out of a besieged city.

In England, small, unmanned hydrogen balloons had been sent off in 1783 by two Italians, Count Francesco Zambeccari and Michael Bigaggni. But these balloons were merely toys. The first British attempt to carry a man into the air was made by an eccentric Scotsman named James Tytler, a failed doctor who had become a chemist's assistant and then a hack writer. With an assistant named Scott (the Edinburgh chemist with whom he worked) he constructed an extremely clumsy montgolfière-type balloon shaped like a barrel, forty feet high and thirty feet wide. The pan on which the fire was lit weighed over three hundred pounds, and the two would-be aeronauts had so much trouble with this that the Edinburgh mob, annoyed by repeated delays, charged the enclosure and destroyed the gallery in which the two men were to have been carried.

But Tytler was a man of courage; determined to prove his claims, he allowed himself to be carried aloft in this dangerous craft, clinging to a rope "like a log or piece of ballast." He managed to do two "leaps" of about five hundred feet before the whole thing collapsed. Attempts to build a second balloon ended in failure, due partly to bad weather conditions and partly to the anger of the mob. Poor Tytler ended his life in obscurity and is said to have been killed when he fell into a salt-pit while drunk. Today he would have been given every encouragement and perhaps have been decorated. But this was the eighteenth century, when scientific experiments were looked on with extreme suspicion by the masses.

In London, in 1784, there lived a handsome young Neapolitan, the Chevalier Vincent Lunardi, who claimed to have been secretary to the Neapolitan Ambassador, although he was probably a clerk. Lunardi had the advantage of good looks and great personal charm. Also he was young, loved gay uniforms, and is said to have been irresistible to women. He had heard of the successes of the Montgolfiers and Professor Charles in Paris, and ardently wished to make a balloon ascent from English

The first aerial voyage in England. Vincent Lunardi taking off from the military grounds, Moorfields, London, September 15th, 1784

soil. Fortunately we possess his own personal account of his attempts to make and then fly in a balloon, published in the form of a series of letters to a friend in Italy. His little book is entitled

An Account of the First Aerial Voyage in England by Vincent Lunardi, Secretary to the Neapolitan Ambassador: To his guardian, Chevalier Gherdo Compagni.

Lunardi begins by making the point that most British men of science and letters seemed far less interested in the "Science of Aerostation" than their French counterparts; in fact, they were downright hostile to it in many cases. When the French successes were announced, the *Morning Herald* suggested that all men "should laugh this new folly out of practice as soon as possible." And after King George III had watched a demonstration of a small hydrogen balloon at Windsor, and had written to Sir Joseph Banks, President of the Royal Society, offering to help finance future similar experiments, he had received this frosty reply: "No good whatever could become of them as the properties by which such a globe acts are as well known as if twenty experiments were made."

So Lunardi, who had no money himself, raised it by first making his balloon, which was over one hundred feet in diameter, and then exhibiting it in a public hall in London called the Lyceum. He charged a sum for admission, but funds were slow coming in. Lunardi and his friend George Biggin, a distinguished amateur scientist who was determined to accompany the Italian on his first flight, had to endure many weeks of frustration.

Meanwhile the balloon, made of silk and divided in alternate gores of red and white, attracted much admiration. So did Signor Lunardi.

Because an earlier attempted balloon flight had ended in mob violence and destruction, Lunardi had great difficulty in finding either a site for his ascension or permission to make it. It looked, for a time, as if the two aspiring aeronauts would have to abandon their attempt. But word got around, particularly among the fashionable visitors to the Lyceum, that the gallant Lunardi and his friend had been disappointed. Lunardi wrote:

My honoured Friend,

I still have hope; for what Philosophers dare not attempt, the Ladies easily accomplish. They can smile into acquiescence that uncouth monster, public prejudice, and they regulate the opinions and manners of a nation at pleasure.

My perseverance, amidst the difficulties and supposed dangers which surround me, the consequence of the failure of de Moret, has given me an air of heroism which you know interests the fair sex. The Lyceum, therefore, is crowded with company, and particularly Ladies, who take for granted I am to ascend; many wish I were not engaged with Mr. Biggin, that they might accompany me; and, with that bewitching air of sincerity which is almost peculiar to the women of this country, and which I think more difficult to resist than the coquetry of my own, they express a tender concern for my safety, which fixes my determination; and I *will* ascend, if I do it from the street. . . .

Vincent Lunardi

The solution of the problem came through Biggin, who introduced Lunardi to friends who were members of the Honourable Artillery Company. They had a parade ground at Moorfields, which offered two advantages. It was spacious enough to accommodate the crowds who would watch the ascent (having paid a guinea for the privilege), and the Honourable Artillery Company could offer protection against the mob, which might attempt to break in if there was a disappointment. After a long discussion the Company voted to permit Lunardi and Biggin to make the attempt in their grounds.

Even so the Neapolitan's troubles were not over. The manager of the Lyceum, which had admitted over 20,000 people to view the balloon, demanded royalties of a considerable amount; when refused, he closed the doors with the balloon inside, refusing access to Lunardi. Lunardi was granted a warrant for the removal of the balloon from the Lyceum, if necessary by force. On September 4th, 1784, the balloon was moved under an armed guard. "Behold me," wrote the agitated Lunardi, "exhausted by fatigue and anxiety and distress at the event of an undertaking that requires my being collected, cool and easy in mind."

Lunardi's balloon was of the hydrogen type, which required long filling, and the work was entrusted to a Dr. Fordyce. It took a very long time, so that although the ascent was scheduled for between noon and 1:00 p.m., the whole of the previous night was occupied by filling the balloon. At 4:00 a.m. Fordyce found all the men responsible for filling the envelope hopelessly drunk, and he himself was in little better condition. Somehow, though, work continued, and on the following day 150,-000 people assembled round the grounds, in addition to the privileged few who were allowed within the grounds.

By two in the afternoon, the balloon was still partly limp, and the roar of the vast assemblage grew menacing. Lunardi decided to delay matters no further and to make the ascent alone. Among the important spectators was the Prince of Wales, the future George IV. His father, George III, broke off his deliberations in Whitehall to watch the event from a distance. He said, "We may resume our deliberations on the subject before us at pleasure. But we may never see poor Lunardi again." So the King and his Prime Minister, William Pitt the Younger, observed the ascent through telescopes.

When the signal was given to cast off, the balloon rose to a considerable height. Lunardi waved flags at the crowd to show that he was well, and then, entranced by the experience, began to eat his provisions, which included some cold chicken and a bottle of champagne. He was accompanied by a dog, a cat, and a pigeon in a cage. The Prince of Wales and the notables, not believing that they would ever see Lunardi again alive, doffed their hats reverently and stood to attention.

But Lunardi was experiencing that euphoria which often comes to balloonists on their first flight. As he floated silently over the fields of Hertfordshire, he experienced, he tells us, "a feeling of calm delight." Later he wrote to his correspondent in Italy:

. . . When the thermometer was at fifty, the effect of the atmosphere and the combination of

47

circumstances around produce a calm delight which is inexpressible and which no situation on earth could give. The stillness, the extent and magnificence of the scene, rendered it highly aweful. My horizon seemed a perfect circle; the terminating line, several hundred miles in circumference . . . the critics imagine, for they seldom speak from experience, that error is an ingredient of every sublime sensation. It was not possible for me to be on Earth in a situation so free from apprehension. I had not the slightest sense of motion from the machine. I knew not whether it was agitated or tranquil, but by the appearance or disappearance of objects on the Earth. I adjusted the furniture and apparatus. I moved to different parts of the gallery, ate, drank and wrote, just as in my study. . . .

Undoubtedly some of these words were written a mile above the earth, on the first aerial voyage ever undertaken in Great Britain, nearly two hundred years ago. Though many such descriptions have been written since, there is a freshness and spontaneity about Lunardi's account which cannot be surpassed, even though it is written in a style which we find stilted and formal.

After a tranquil journey lasting some one and a half hours, Lunardi's balloon came to rest in a field in Hertfordshire. The cat, which had shown signs of reaction to the cold, was landed. Lunardi also threw overboard his knives and forks, his empty champagne bottle, and other ballast. Thus relieved, he was able to take off again and attain his maximum altitude, finally descending in a large field near Ware. Several farm workers

The flight that never took place! Lunardi intended to take up both his friend George Biggin and the actress Mrs Sage but unfortunately the balloon would not lift all three. So Biggin and Mrs Sage were sent off alone from St. Georges Fields, June 29th, 1785

saw him but were too terrified to come to his assistance. He was eventually saved by a woman, who, with the practicality of her sex, seized the rope he flung out and tethered the balloon to the earth. The men then shame-facedly followed her. Soon they were toasting his health at the Bull Inn at Ware. There is in that field a monu-ment, which survives to this day, commemorating Vin-cent Lunardi and his achievement.

On September 30th, 1784, Horace Walpole, witty and cultivated son of a former Prime Minister, wrote to a friend:

> An Italian, one Lunardi, is the first *airgonaut* that has mounted into the clouds in this country. So far from respecting him as a Jason, I was very angry with him; he had full right to venture his own neck, but none to risk the poor cat, who, not having proved a martyr, is at least better en-titled to be a confessor than her master Daedalus. I was even disappointed *after* his expedition had been prosperous; you must know, I have no ideas of space; when I heard how wonderfully he had soared, I concluded he had arrived within a stone's throw of the moon—alas! he had not as-cended above a mile and a half; so pitiful an ascension degraded him totally in my conceit. As there are mountains twice as high, what signifies flying, if you do not rise above the top of the earth? Any one on foot may walk higher than this man-eagle!

Chapter 3

Experiments and developments

During the late eighteenth century and early nineteenth century, serious aeronauts became more and more concerned with the possibility of making long flights in balloons. They argued that if an ascent was made when the wind was in a certain direction, it might be possible to travel much farther than the earliest aerial travellers had ventured. One such pioneer was Jean-Pierre Blanchard, whose name has already been mentioned. Blanchard possessed considerable courage and initiative, and it was he who conceived the idea of being the first man to cross the English Channel by balloon. In this attempt he was accompanied and financed by an American physician, Dr. John Jeffries of Boston, who, in November 1784, had made an ascent from London in order to measure air pressures at great heights.

Tests in 1784 with unmanned balloons proved that the Channel could be crossed. A balloon sent up from Sandwich in Kent landed at Lille two and a half hours later, and another, which ascended from Canterbury, was picked up at Ypres in Belgium. Early the following year Blanchard and Jeffries were ready to make the attempt. The ascent was made on January 7th, 1785, from Dover Castle, an appropriate site for such a momentous occasion. Dover's mediaeval fortress, the historical "Gateway to England," contains within its walls one of the oldest buildings in the British Isles, the Roman *pharos*, or lighthouse. It must have been from this tower that the Romans watched the passage of their galleys and warships to and from Boulogne nearly 2,000 years ago. Now, within the same enclosure, man was to prove his ability to cross the Channel by air.

But jealousy, spite, and treachery marred the occasion. Blanchard resented the idea of sharing the glory of the flight with a companion. So he deliberately weighted himself with lead (worn in a belt round his waist) in order to weigh down the balloon so that Jeffries would stand down and let him make the flight alone. But Jeffries discovered the trick; the belt was removed, and the American took his seat in the car slug beneath the balloon. The flight was further endangered by Blanchard's insistence that he could control it, and he encumbered the car with wings, a rudder, and a kind of propeller, all of which were quite useless.

The balloon took off from the enclosure of the Castle (which stands on the edge of the cliffs) and rose rather sluggishly. A huge crowd cheered as it set off, blown eastward by the wind across the wave-tops. The balloon struggled up to a height of a few hundred feet above the sea. It might have risen to a much greater height but for the useless gear which encumbered it. Twice during the crossing it dipped so low that the aeronauts were compelled to throw out their ballast; and, when this proved insufficient, they stripped off their clothes and threw these overboard also. Here is part of an account written by Dr. Jeffries:

At about five or six miles from the French coast we were again falling rapidly towards the

The balloonist Jean-Pierre Blanchard described as, "a petulant little fellow, not many inches over five feet, and physically well suited for vapourish regions."

sea, on which occasion my noble little captain [Blanchard] gave orders, and set the example, by beginning to strip our aerial car, first of our silk and finery; this not giving us sufficient release, we cast one wing, then the other; after which I was obliged to unscrew and cast away our *moulinet* [propeller]; yet, still approaching the sea very fast, and the boats being much alarmed for us, we cast away first one anchor, then the other, after which my little hero stripped and threw away his coat. On this, I was compelled to follow his example. He next threw away his trowsers [it was January] . . . . Luckily at this instant we found the mercury beginning to fall in the barometer and we soon ascended much higher than ever before, and made a most beautiful entrée into France at three o'clock.

We entered rising, and to such a height that the arch we described brought us down just twelve miles into the country, when we descended most tranquilly, into the forest of *De Felmores*, almost as naked as the trees, not an inch of cord or rope left, no anchor or anything to help us, nor a being within several miles.

About half an hour later, footmen and horsemen arrived on the scene, Blanchard and Jeffries having managed to let sufficient hydrogen out of the balloon to prevent it from taking off again. Jeffries tells us that he "was soon well mounted and had a fine gallop of seven miles" to the château of a Monsieur de Saudrouin, who, after entertaining the aeronauts lavishly, sent them on to Calais "in an elegant chariot and six horses." To this day, the car of their balloon is preserved in the Calais Museum, and Blanchard was awarded a prize of 12,000 *livres* by Louis XVI. Jeffries got nothing.

Blanchard's success in crossing the Channel inspired others to attempt the same journey. Among these was Pilâtre de Rozier, who, with the Marquis d'Arlandes, had made the first successful aerial voyage.

Pilâtre de Rozier had considered the relative advantages of the hydrogen and hot-air balloons. The montgolfière in which he and d'Arlandes had made their ascent from Versailles could not rise as high or as swiftly as the hydrogen balloon of Professor Charles. On the other hand, it appeared to be more sensitive to control, for by adding only a little fuel to the fire under the neck of the balloon he could make it rise quickly; if the fire was allowed to die down, it descended. The young aeronaut, having studied the record of Blanchard's performance, conceived the idea that, if he could maintain his craft at a certain height and gain the advantage of the prevailing air currents at that height, he could make a swift and certain crossing, even though the prevailing cross-Channel winds are from the west, whereas he proposed to make the journey from the east, embarking at Boulogne and landing in England.

There was an additional hazard in this attempt: an aeronaut attempting to cross from England to the Continent had all Europe to land in, whereas anyone trying to fly westward, if he was blown off course, would find himself over the bleak and lonely Atlantic. Added to this was the greatest risk of all: Pilâtre de Rozier calmly proposed to combine both types of balloon—the hydrogen balloon, a ball of highly inflammable gas, suspended above a montgolfière, under which a fire was kept perpetually burning.

Professor Charles, well aware of the danger, said that Pilâtre de Rozier was risking his life in proposing "to light his fire beside his powder magazine." Nevertheless, the young man went ahead with his scheme, and the great balloon was constructed in readiness for the take-off from Boulogne. It was a cumbersome construction, to which the French government had contributed the sum of 1,600 *livres*. The wind blew constantly from the west, not the east, and the balloon was severely damaged before takeoff.

In the meantime, Pilâtre de Rozier had fallen in love with a young English girl who was staying in a convent in the town. It was agreed between them that they were to marry at the successful ending of the venture.

Day after day, Pilâtre de Rozier scanned the horizon, hoping for a change in the direction of the wind. To make matters worse, the Controller of Finances, de

55

Calonne, reproached him for the delays, upbraiding him in brutal terms. On the eve of his departure, a French aristocrat, the Marquis de Maisonfort, threw a roll of 200 *louis* into the car in the hope that Pilâtre de Rozier would take him as companion, as he had taken the Marquis d'Arlandes. But the aeronaut replied sternly, "This experiment is too uncertain to risk the life of another," and refused the bribe.

On June 15th, 1785, at seven in the morning, Pilâtre de Rozier rose from the ground in his combined balloons, from one of which the gas was escaping at several points. At the last moment he had been persuaded to take one of his workmen, named Romain, along. Conditions were by no means ideal, and Pilâtre de Rozier, trying to find a current that would carry him across the Channel, rose to about 3,000 feet. He was still over land when horrified onlookers saw the balloon shrouded in smoke. The boom of an explosion followed, a second or two later, as the car and its occupants were seen plummeting to earth. When the search party reached the spot, they found Pilâtre de Rozier dead and horribly mutilated. Romain was still alive but died shortly afterwards. It is not said whether the young English girl betrothed to Pilâtre de Rozier watched the ascent and saw the catastrophe; she probably did.

Thus balloon flight had claimed its first victims. The French public, which had taken Pilâtre de Rozier to its heart, was deeply shocked, and there were no more experiments for some time afterwards.

The early days of ballooning—and indeed the whole century following the invention of the balloon—were marked by a determination to find some way of directing flight. Many silly ideas were put forward, one of which was to harness eagles or even pigeons to the craft.

The first Channel crossing by air by Jean-Pierre Blanchard and
Dr. John Jeffries, January 7th, 1785

Other ideas were not so silly. Joseph Montgolfier,
indeed, anticipated the principle of jet propulsion. He
helped two priests, Miollan and Janinet, to construct
a balloon ninety-two feet broad and one hundred feet
high. It was based on the montgolfière principle—that
is, was filled with hot air produced by a fire below the

neck. But Montgolfier introduced a novel idea: a small hole, only fourteen inches wide, in the *side* of the balloon, through which the hot air would escape, thus driving the machine forward. (Another version has it that there were four holes equally spaced around the sides, with valves to open and close them.) It probably would not have worked but was not even given a chance. The mob, infuriated by the long delay in getting the craft airborne, destroyed it, and the two priests were lucky to escape with their lives.

A less happy idea was to mount small cannons in the car, in the hope that their recoil would drive the balloon forwards. Happily this experiment was never tried, as it would almost certainly have ended in disaster.

Other inventors took ships as their models. For more than 5,000 years, and probably longer, men had been able to control the direction of boats by either sails or oars or by a combination of both. Since air was a fluid medium, like water, why shouldn't sails, oars, and rudders be used in balloons? What these inventors didn't understand is that air is much thinner than water and that a vehicle therefore needs much *greater* propulsive power in air than in water. Moreover, the power of the winds was so great and a balloon presented such a large surface to them that, compared with such power, men hauling on oars—even large ones—would be helpless. Joseph Montgolfier, who was interested in such experiments, pointed out that even in absolutely still air the most powerful aerial oars, operated by human muscles, could only propel the vehicle at about five miles per hour and that the air was rarely still anyway.

Sails and rudders, which were tried for a time, proved

equally futile because—obviously, it seems now—a balloon was itself a sail and would be carried along by the wind in whichever direction it happened to be blowing. And rudders, operating in such a thin medium as air, would have only a slight effect. The next solution offered was the propeller, or airscrew; Blanchard's *moulinet* (windmill) was an example of this. But an airscrew lacking mechanical power, which had to be turned by men operating wheels and pulleys, was insufficiently powerful to influence the flight of a balloon except in absolutely calm air. Nevertheless, the men who thought of the propeller correctly anticipated the method which was, eventually, to drive first dirigibles (controlled balloons) and later powered aircraft, until the invention of the jet engine.

When the reciprocal steam engine was invented, towards the end of the eighteenth century, men naturally considered applying this power to driving propellers, but it proved too heavy for the balloon to lift.

The principle of streamlining was understood nearly two hundred years ago. It was soon realized that the spherical balloon offered too much resistance to the air, and efforts were made to improve its shape. The Academy of Dijon took a lead in this matter and commissioned Guyton de Morveau to design a machine of which the front was wedge-shaped, to offer minimum resistance to the air, while steering was to be done by means of a vertical sail erected at the other end. But to no avail; this and other experiments failed since the machine could not be flown against the wind, but had to follow it.

Another experiment introduced small air bags, or ballonets, into the envelope; the idea, which we owe to a mathematician and military man named Jean-Baptiste Meusnier de la Place, was to enable the designers to make elongated craft of more streamlined shape. The first of such balloons designed by him was shaped like an egg. Others had pointed ends similar to those of the Zeppelins of the First World War. The bags were filled with ordinary atmospheric air, while the rest of the envelope contained either hydrogen or some other inflammable gas (such as coal gas) or hot air provided by the usual montgolfière fire at the base.

It was in an egg-shaped balloon of this design that the Robert brothers, accompanied by the Duc de Chartres (later Philippe Egalité) and others, ascended from Versailles not long after Pilâtre de Rozier and the Marquis d'Arlandes had made their first successful flight. The attempt nearly ended fatally. Shortly after leaving the ground, the "aeronauts . . . felt the necessity of getting rid of a globe of which no use whatever could be made; but in attempting to get hold of it they let it fall in so bungling a manner that it stopped the orifice left open for the escape of gas. Fearing an explosion, the Duc de Chartres took it upon himself to make a hole in the balloon. Some say he did this with his sword." *

The balloon's abiding weakness was that whatever power was generated (before the coming of the internal-combustion engine in the late nineteenth century) was still too feeble to counteract the effect of strong air currents. The balloon remained at their mercy, and the long-distance flights made in the nineteenth century (some of which were remarkable) were achieved only by taking advantage of prevailing winds. The air currents, not the balloon, provided the motive power.

* W. de Fonvielle, *Adventures in the Air* (London, 1877).

Chapter 4

The world's first
air force

It was not long before the new invention was put to military use. The possibility of using the balloon for watching the movement of troops on the ground was soon recognized, and what might be described as the first air force in the world was organized as far back as the time of the French Revolution.

Having guillotined the King and Queen of France, together with hundreds of their aristocratic supporters, the new republic found itself surrounded by formidable enemies such as Holland, Austria, and Great Britain. The ill-trained Republican armies, spread over a wide front, had to meet the onslaught of highly skilled professional armies. But the Republican troops and their leaders had a burning faith in their revolutionary cause and were ready to accept new ideas. One of these ideas was the military use of the balloon.

In 1793 one of the first acts of the Committee of Public Safety, established after the execution of Louis XVI, was to establish a committee of scientists for the express purpose of encouraging scientific invention, particularly if it would help the cause of the Revolution.

One of the aeronauts thus enlisted was Louis-Bernard Guyton de Morveau, who had experimented with coal gas as a lifting agent and had tried various means of making a balloon controllable, though without success. If Guyton de Morveau had succeeded in this aim, he would have revolutionized warfare and almost certainly would have won the war for France; but he had the good sense to realize that for the time being it would be best to concentrate on the military potentialities of the balloon as it then existed. These would be mainly in the field of aerial reconnaissance: looking down from a captive balloon on troop concentrations and reporting their movement and positions.

From the start, Guyton de Morveau ran into difficulties, one of which was the fact that the Committee of Public Safety, the body which effectively governed France, forbade him to use sulphuric acid to make hydrogen, all the available sulphur being needed to make gunpowder. He enlisted the help of one of Professor Charles' former pupils, a Colonel Coutelle. With Coutelle he devised a different method of producing hydrogen—the decomposition of water, which is, of course, a combination of hydrogen and oxygen. The method they devised was fairly simple but slow in operation.

If steam, vaporized water, is brought into contact with red-hot metal, the metal combines with the oxygen to form an oxide, and the hydrogen is released. So the two experimenters allowed water to flow from an upper reservoir through a pipe to which a narrow jet was fixed. The water naturally vaporized, and the steam, forced down by the weight of the water above it, came into contact with the red-hot metal (iron filings), and the hydrogen was drawn off through another pipe to fill the balloon.

The first experiments, watched by the committee of scientists, took place in Paris. When 18,000 cubic feet of hydrogen had been produced, Colonel Coutelle went to General Jourdan, who was in command of the besieged city of Maubeuge, and asked him to allow the necessary material for the balloon's inflation to be sent to him from Paris. But Jourdan, a conventional soldier unfamiliar with the latest scientific developments, was suspicious of Coutelle, failed to understand what he was talking about, and threatened to shoot him as a spy.

Eventually the matter was straightened out, and Jourdan congratulated Coutelle on his enterprise in the defence of his country. But he recommended that if such an experiment were to be made it must be at some place other than Maubeuge, which was too closely besieged. So the world's first military balloon was flown over Paris, with Coutelle in the observation basket. The balloon rose to a height of about 2,100 feet above the Seine, and from that height it was not easy to pick out and identify with precision objects covering an area of something like 1,100 square miles. Aerial observers have to be trained both to observe and to report, and Coutelle, being a pioneer, could have had no training, so his was not an easy task. However, the Seine helped him to get his bearings, and he was able, with the aid of a powerful telescope, to distinguish all its windings as far as Meulan, sixteen miles away. He also exchanged some sort of signals, perhaps by means of a prearranged code, with the ground, thus proving the utility of the balloon for military observation. He felt so overwhelmed and overpowered by this experience that he later insisted that an observation officer should always have an assistant with him.

The next step was to put the new technique into practice. Coutelle visited General Jourdan again, and now found him quite accommodating. It was agreed that a permanent Balloon Corps be established near the town of Meudon, where regular training could be given. This corps, established in 1793, was known as *Les Aérostiers* and was the embryo of the world's first air force. Like the air forces of today, it contained a large proportion of officers and men who did not conform to the normal military pattern. For instance, among the officers there were a former priest from Montmorency and a master mason named Delaunay, whom Coutelle used because he was skilled in the construction of furnaces, and who was commissioned as a lieutenant. Another officer who rose from the ranks was Selles de Beauchamp, who enlisted under the name Chevalier Albert. When a child of six, de Beauchamp lost his father, and two years later his mother also died. The orphan was educated at Harcourt College as a "young man of quality." His tutor eagerly embraced the revolutionary cause, but de Beauchamp stuck to the Court party. Attempting to escape from France, he was arrested and sent to join the Army of the Loire, but rather than do this he enlisted as a military balloonist, and it is to his memoirs that we owe most of our knowedge of the Balloon Corps.

The training centre was eventually commanded by a young man named Nicolas-Jacques Conté, who, like many distinguished men of this revolutionary epoch, was the son of poor peasants. He was born near Sées, in the *département* of Orne, and two priests who liked the child took his education in hand. He was still little more than a schoolboy when the Montgolfiers' balloon made its first historic flight. Two years later, a lawyer from Alençon tried to send up a balloon but failed. Young Conté stepped in, made some adjustments and modifications, and the next ascent was successful. The lawyer, impressed by the lad's intelligence and ingenuity, provided the means for him to complete his education.

The manner in which Conté came to the notice of the French revolutionary authorities is typical of the atmosphere of that period. He happened to be passing when Coutelle was attempting a second inflation in Paris, before setting out for Meudon. Observing the slow, cumbersome process, he made some critical comments to a passer-by. This man took it on himself to follow Conté and find out where he lived. Then he passed the information on to the celebrated General Lazare Carnot. Carnot sent for Conté, questioned him shrewdly, and, recognizing his high talent, gave him a post connected with the inflation of balloons. Later, when Conté became famous, Napoleon said of him that "he has all the sciences in his head, and all the arts at his fingertips."

Members of *Les Aérostiers* wore the normal uniform of the military engineers of the period, the officers being rather magnificent in their gold-braided tunics, knee-breeches, epaulettes, and three-cornered hats. But all members bore a special distinguishing mark: their copper buttons were engraved with the figure of a balloon. Each company consisted of fifty men, a miscellaneous collection of lawyers, merchants, clerks, and students, but all proud of their position as *aérostiers*. Those buttons meant that they shared something of the glory of Pilâtre de Rozier and the Montgolfiers.

There were no sergeant-pilots or other non-commissioned ranks among the men who flew in the balloons;

they were invariably officers. But most of the *aérostiers* were concerned with inflating the balloons, maintaining and repairing them, and getting them into the air and down again. The construction and maintenance of the furnaces for making hydrogen was itself a major operation. In their role, these men resembled the extensive ground crews that enable modern pilots to fly. De Beauchamp notes in his memoirs that during this time the men responsible took hardly any sleep.

General Jourdan changed his mind about not allowing Coutelle to send a balloon up from the city of Maubeuge. Although Maubeuge was being besieged by the Austrians and the Dutch, the Balloon Corps managed to take in their apparatus and fly their first balloon, named the *Entreprenant,* from inside the city. The technique of operation was roughly as follows: The inflated balloon, carrying two officers and a certain amount of ballast, would rise to a height of 1,650 feet. It could not rise any higher because of the weight of the strong cables used to hold it against a powerful wind. The ballast was thrown out as the balloon rose, in order to counteract the weight of these cables.

> The first ascent was made amid the thunder of cannon and the "hurrahs" of the garrison. If we may believe the report made after the descent by the engineer officer who accompanied Colonel Coutelle, it was impossible for the enemy to make a single movement without every detail becoming known. The officer pretended to have been able to count the number of panes in windows of houses at a distance of fifteen miles. This is possible enough, no doubt, in very clear

weather, though we are inclined to believe that the officer was exaggerating.

The moral effect produced in the Austrian camp by this spectacle, so novel and unexpected, was immense. The commanders soon perceived that their soldiers believed they had to deal with sorcerers. To combat this dangerous opinion, and restore their courage, the Austrian general resolved to destroy, at any cost, this fatal machine. *

Unlike the observation balloons known in the 1914–1918 war and later, the *Entreprenant* had to make its ascent very close to the enemy lines, and always from the same place, within the courtyard of a college. So the enemy gunners, observing this, placed two four-pound guns in a nearby hollow, and one morning, as the *Entreprenant* made its majestic ascent with Colonel Coutelle in the car, these guns opened fire at close range. One cannonball barely cleared the balloon, and another grazed the bottom of the car, whereupon Colonel Coutelle stood to attention, saluted, and shouted "Vive la République!" He then gave the signal for the ascent to continue and was soon out of range of the enemy guns. Feats such as this endeared the *aérostiers* to the French public.

The Balloon Corps of the republican army had to cope with problems which no military force had encountered before. One of them was transporting the *Entreprenant*. After the relief of Maubeuge, they had to take it some forty miles to Charleroi in Belgium, which was held by the enemy. In order to preserve the

---

* From an account, based on de Beauchamp's memoirs, in W. de Fonvielle, *Adventures in the Air* (London, 1877).

Early balloon reconnaissance by the French at the battle of Fleurus by the balloon *Entreprenant* on June 26th, 1794

precious hydrogen, which took so long to produce, it was decided to maintain the balloon inflated, and carry it aloft when the army moved. To deceive the enemy, they left the road and transported their precious balloon across open country. It was an extremely hot summer and the *aérostiers*, nearly naked on account of the heat, and covered with coal dust (since they were moving through mining country), looked more like devils than men. Above them floated the balloon, an object of superstitious dread and wonder among the peasantry and miners through whose villages they passed. Food was left for them at convenient halting places, and at times their comrades of the regular army denied themselves their own rations in order to assist the *aérostiers*.

The *Entreprenant* was a "secret weapon," something new and terrifying, an aerial spy which could rise high above the enemy and give away all their military movements. The French generals realized this. Just as the Balloon Corps were nearing the end of their laborious journey, a cloud of dust rose as the general-in-chief and his entire staff galloped up to do them honour. There was a universal "hurrah" from officers and soldiers. Then, headed by a military band, the whole cortege conducted the balloon to its headquarters in an abandoned farm. Next morning the *Entreprenant* rose high into the sky, amid a deafening noise of artillery, and that evening the enemy city capitulated.

The balloon was used again at the battle of Fleurus in Belgium. On this occasion the officer in command, General Morlot, collaborated closely with Colonel Coutelle. Questions were sent up by means of a cord and answers sent down attached to small bags of ballast. The *Entreprenant* was up for ten hours, during which every enemy movement was under close observation.

Just how effective was the balloon as an aerial spy? Probably less than its users thought at the time. But its effect on morale was undoubtedly great. De Beauchamp tells how a soldier of a French brigade, dissatisfied with an order to quit the field of battle, shouted, "Would the balloon be with us if we were really on the point of leaving the battlefield?" Thus encouraged, the brigade fought on and won. Two days later the French entered Brussels in triumph, towing the balloon with them. So impressed was the French government that it ordered the formation of a second company of *aérostiers* at Meudon.

Again, in 1795, the company of balloonists assisted at the siege of Mainz, where Coutelle gained high honour. At first the Austrians asked for an armistice, though this was almost certainly to give them an opportunity to view the balloon at close quarters. But then, when negotiations were broken off, a fierce wind arose, so powerful that the combined efforts of sixty-four men were not sufficient to hold down the balloon; they were lifted off their feet. The Austrians, seeing the difficulty which Coutelle was facing, sent an officer with a flag of truce, begging the aeronaut to cease exposing himself to danger —an interesting comparison of eighteenth-century warfare with that of today. Colonel Coutelle refused, and survived.

Why, then, after all these successes, was military ballooning virtually abandoned by the French after the rise of Napoleon? Part of the answer may lie in the conservatism of the professional soldier, who prefers old and well-tried methods. (It is said that Marshall Haig, who commanded British troops during part of the 1914–1918 war, at first regarded aeroplanes as little better than toys.) But most of the answer must lie in the difficulty of passing adequate information to the ground from an altitude of 2,000 feet before the telephone and radio were invented. The eighteenth-century military balloonist was ahead of his time. If photography had been in use, the story would have been very different.

Whatever the reason or reasons, military ballooning practically ceased in France after 1798, when the First Company of Aérostiers was sent to Egypt in Napoleon's ill-fated invasion of that country. After their equipment had been destroyed by the British Fleet at the battle of Aboukir, Bonaparte ordered that they be disbanded, and the military balloon suffered a decline until the American Civil War, nearly seventy years later.

Chapter 5

Ballooning for excitement

Up to this point, the end of the eighteenth century, we have been looking at the great feats of ballooning in the order in which they happened. Now we have to take separately the development of the balloon, first as a piece of popular entertainment, second as a military device, and third as a means by which eminent men of science attempted to explore the upper atmosphere. It is necessary to make this distinction because to consider the three elements together would be confusing.

From about 1800 onwards, ballooning became more and more popuar with the masses. The public loved to watch or take part in balloon ascents for the fun and novelty of it, and a generation of showmen-aeronauts grew up who made ascents from fairgrounds and from places of popular entertainment such as Vauxhall Gardens, the Cremorne Gardens, and the Crystal Palace in London. They gave balloon rides to thousands. As a distinguished Victorian scientist, James Glaisher, F.R.S., expressed it in his book *Travels in the Air* (1871):

> The comparatively easy management of a balloon . . . in the hands of a practised aeronaut, under whose guidance for a matter of a small fee

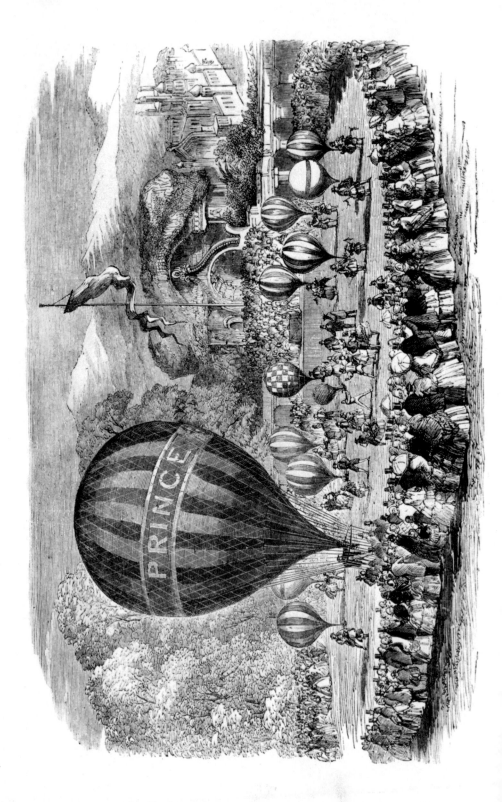

one can sit securely and for an hour or two enjoy the delight of aerial voyage within sight of earth, is one reason, I believe, why the balloon has gradually degenerated into an instrument of popular exhibition and passing amusement, so that its striking characteristics and important bearing on science are in danger of fading completely out of view.

This sounds pompous, but one must remember that Glaisher and men like him were seriously concerned because too little attention was being paid to the possibilities of using the balloon to explore the higher regions of the atmosphere.

Meanwhile, ignoring scientific ascents, we shall see how, throughout the nineteenth century, balloons were used for the sport of enthusiasts and as a source of wonder and excitement for millions of ordinary people who thronged to see them at public gardens and other places of entertainment. During that century, thousands of balloon ascents were made throughout Europe and America, and the great balloon pilots were as popular in their day as racing-car drivers are in ours.

Like racing-car drivers, they hazarded their lives, and there were many tragedies. The great Blanchard, for instance, having originally made his name as the first aeronaut to cross the English Channel, went on to make numerous ascents from the main cities of Europe. On November 19th, 1785, before the outbreak of the French Revolution, he had one of the narrowest escapes of his career. In an ascent from Ghent, in Belgium, having miscalculated the amount of ballast he would need to achieve a steady climb, he shot up like a rocket and soon found himself at a height which he estimated (from the barometer) as 32,000 feet, nearly six miles.

The bitter cold of those upper regions immediately affected him. Ice formed on the basket and on Blanchard's clothing. Though half-paralyzed and nearly unconscious, he had the quickness of mind to realize that he would not have the strength to hold on to the line controlling the valve long enough for the gas to escape and halt his upward flight. So, without hesitation, he ripped open the balloon, and the collapsed envelope, streaming upwards in tatters, began to plunge earthwards.

When he neared the ground, Blanchard, realizing the furious speed of his descent, darted up into the hoop above the car, clung to the ropes, and so saved his life. The car, hitting the earth first, broke his fall, and he survived.

As Blanchard was alone, with no companion to bear out his statements, some scientists refused to believe that he had attained so great a height; but the experiences of a later generation of aeronauts, who ascended even higher under controlled conditions, suggest that he was telling the truth.

He went on making ascents; and, to divert the crowd with novelties, he had the not very happy idea of sending his dog and other animals down attached to miniature parachutes. When the revolutionary wars broke out, Blanchard happened to be in the Tyrol with his balloon. On the pretext that he was trying to spread "republican principles," he was thrown into jail. On his release he went to America, and was the first man to make a balloon ascent in the United States, watched, in 1793, by the President, George Washington.

Mention of the parachute reminds us that, though Blanchard did eventually descend by parachute himself, he was not the first to do so, although he claimed to be the inventor. The idea of the parachute goes back several hundred years; Leonardo da Vinci made a drawing of one which would probably have worked. But the first man to entrust himself to a parachute was a Frenchman named André-Jacques Garnerin, who was born in 1769. A pupil of the celebrated Professor Charles, he was nineteen when he made his first balloon ascent "accompanied by a lady of Tumerman." (By this time a number of women had emulated Madame Thible, the first woman to fly, including a Mrs. Sage, who accompanied Lunardi on one of his flights from England.)

Later, while serving gallantly with the French Army, Garnerin was captured by the British, who handed him over to the Austrians. They imprisoned him in Budapest, and it was there, he tells us, that he first had the idea of making a parachute—for the purpose of escaping. On being released, he pursued this idea. His eventual design was not unlike a modern parachute except that it had a little car for the aeronaut, shaped rather like a Davy safety lamp, hung beneath it. This parachute with car he attached to his balloon, instead of the normal car, and ascended from Paris on June 18th, 1797. After reaching a certain height (not stated) he cut the attaching rope and at the same time operated a device which ripped open the balloon. The parachute swung to and fro so wildly that Garnerin was in danger of being flung out, but he held on and landed safe but shaken. Later the astronomer Joseph-Jérôme de Lalande suggested a simple modification which made the parachute more manageable: a hole in the top, allowing

The world's first parachute descent from the air by André-Jacques Garnerin on October 22nd, 1797, over Paris

some of the air to spill out, so that the parachute did not swing so violently during the descent. Later a still better answer to this problem was discovered: to make the parachute of material sufficiently porous to allow a certain amount of air to escape.

Having applauded Lunardi, the British became equally enthralled by Garnerin, who in 1802 repeated,

over London, his successful parachute descent over
Paris. Ascending from St. George's Parade, North Audley
Street, he rose to 10,000 feet before releasing himself
from the balloon. This time, owing to the much greater
height, the parachute swung even more wildly, and
many of the spectators feared that the French aeronaut
had been killed. But he was found in a field near St.
Pancras, sick and bruised, but otherwise unhurt.

One of the popular ballad-writers of the time commemorated Garnerin's descent in these words:

> Bold Garnerin went up
> Which increased his repute
> And came safe to earth
> In his Grand Parachute.

Garnerin's wife, Jeanne-Geneviève, and his beautiful niece, Eliza, both made many descents, and on one
occasion, in Spain, when the balloon failed to take off,
Eliza and her father were flung into jail. Though released
after a short time, Eliza hated King Ferdinand so much
that on her return to France she wrote a pamphlet ac-
cusing him of unjust treatment and demanding an
apology. She got it. The King lamely said that he had
put the aeronauts into custody to protect them from
the fury of the mob.

To get this matter in perspective, one should remember that it was in this period that the great English
novelist Jane Austen was writing her novels, in which
some of her heroines, no doubt drawn from life, are
delicate, demure creatures fluttering their fans at the
approach of a man and fainting or reaching for their
smelling-salts on any emotional occasion. Yet, as these
novels were being written, women were plunging from

77

10,000 feet in primitive parachutes and doing what few men, even in the twentieth century, would like to attempt.

Garnerin, in his normal balloon flights, was often accompanied by women. One of these journeys, when he shared the car with a Mademoiselle Célestine Henry, he ran into unexpected trouble on approaching the ground. The balloon was pursued by two mounted policemen, who shouted to the aeronauts, "Your passports! Your passports!" Neither had a passport, and on landing they were arrested. The official responsible, subjected to much leg-pulling, soon released his prisoners. After that Garnerin always carried a passport giving him admittance to any European country to which the balloon might carry him.

Bad luck often followed these pioneer aeronauts. At one moment they were the darlings of the crowds; at the next they were objects of suspicion. Garnerin, for example, who became extremely popular because of his courage, charm, and technical skill, had the ill fortune to fall foul of Napoleon. In 1804 he was put in charge of the aeronautical part of the celebrations which commemorated the crowning of Napoleon as Emperor of France. He supervised the construction of a magnificent balloon which was to rise above the roofs of Paris, unmanned, but adorned by a crown made up of 3,000 lamps representing the imperial crown which His Holiness the Pope had placed on the head of Napoleon.

No compliment could have been more magnificent, and it might be thought that this alone would have won high honours for the designer of the balloon. Alas, this was not so, owing to an unlucky, million-to-one chance. The unpiloted balloon was carried by steady winds all the way from Paris to *Rome itself*, the very capital in which the new Emperor had been crowned. Why un-lucky? Because the balloon, instead of either continuing its journey or landing in a suitable place, chose to hit the tomb of that infamous tyrant the Emperor Nero, and there the crown stuck.

Napoleon, like many despots, lacked a sense of humour, and was extremely superstitious. He was enraged when certain newspapers printed some very sarcastic comments on this coincidence, and became convinced that Garnerin had done it deliberately. It was in vain that the luckless aeronaut pleaded that he was not re-sponsible for where the balloon landed, since it was unpiloted. Napoleon, despite being a member of the Academy of Sciences, distrusted balloons. He never forgave Garnerin, who fell into deep disgrace.

In the meantime Garnerin's principal rival, Jean-Pierre Blanchard, continued to make adventurous as-cents for many years. During his fifty-fifth flight, made from Lyon, he rose so high that the valve at the top of the balloon, used to release gas when the aeronaut wished to descend, froze solid, and it took all Blanchard's efforts to free it. He was in the air for five hours, mostly at a very high altitude, but by reason of the cross-winds which played with the balloon, he descended not very far from where he started.

In 1808, Blanchard made an ascent from the castle of the King of Holland, near the Hague. He had scarcely left the ground when he was seized by apoplexy, and was unable to control the balloon. It fell from the height of a mere sixty feet, flinging him to the ground. Al-though he survived for a time, the concussion produced by the fall affected his mind, and he lay in the hospital, mentally deranged. He worried incessantly about his wife, since the pension which the late King Louis XVI had granted him after his cross-Channel flight had been cancelled, as had all state pensions awarded by the former King of France. Almost his last words to his wife were: "My poor dear, when I am dead, I fear you will have no other resources than to throw yourself into the Seine." But Madame Blanchard was made of sterner stuff, as we shall see. Blanchard died on March 7th, 1809.

Madame Blanchard, far from throwing herself into the Seine after her husband's death, decided to become an aeronaut herself. She was a tough little woman with a sallow skin and a sharp, bird-like face, immensely determined and very brave. This is not to say that she was without fear, for, according to people who knew her, she was so nervous that driving in a coach terrified her —she was always afraid that it would overturn. She was also extremely sensitive to noise and hated crowds. Yet she would take off alone, in the car of her balloon, usually at night, and after firing off Bengal lights and other fireworks to amuse the multitude, settle down for a night's sleep, while the balloon floated on through the darkness, to land she knew not where.

Wherever she appeared, she drew enormous crowds, not only in Paris but in Berlin, Vienna, Rome, London —wherever there was money to be made, and she made quite a lot. Like her late husband, she had several narrow escapes from death. On one occasion she permitted her balloon to go too high and was almost frozen to death by a cloud of ice crystals which stuck to her face. Then, in 1818, when quite close to the ground, she opened the release valve too quickly, fell into a tree, and remained perched in its topmost branches until some peasants rescued her.

On July 7th, 1819, she made a spectacular ascent, by night, from the Tivoli Gardens in Paris. Orchestras played; ladies and gentlemen sat at tables overlooking the green lawns or strolled arm in arm along the tree-lined avenues, softly lit by lanterns. Every kind of amusement was to be had. For the rich and well-to-do, there were opera singers and orchestral concerts and a ballroom. For the poorer, there were the usual fairground entertainments. As the time of Madame Blanchard's ascent drew near, the ladies and gentlemen left their tables, the crowds began to desert the fairground, and all those thousands concentrated around the space, cleared and guarded, from which the great balloon was to ascend. Many coloured lights illuminated the enclosure above which the huge envelope of the balloon swayed in the wind, held down by ropes in the hands of many assistants.

A continuous murmur went up while the crowd waited for the tiny figure of Madame Blanchard to climb into the aerial car. When at last she appeared, tripping across the grass with small but determined steps, the murmur swelled to a roar; men threw their hats in the air; thousands clapped and shouted, "Bon voyage!" Madame Blanchard turned and curtsied before being assisted into the car.

I will let de Fonvielle tell the rest of the story:

A bombshell gave the signal for ascent. The trees were suddenly illuminated by Bengal lights. Madame Blanchard ascended to the sound of brilliant music. The balloon drew after it an immense star which had been lighted. Faggots like those which were burning in the garden were lit, and the balloon illuminated by mysterious fires glided across the sky like a passing meteor.

Soon there falls a shower of gold which seems to come from the car. Frantic applause from below reaches the ear of Madame Blanchard. The brave aeronaut is seen to stoop; she lights a bomb of silver rain, which being suspended to a parachute, descends with supernatural majesty.

Unfortunately the balloon, which always continues to ascend, allows quantities of gas to escape. A jet of gas is lit by a stick of fireworks. A train of fire shoots out; the balloon is in flames. An enormous tongue of flame issues from it. From all parts below, the plaudits are redoubled.

But Madame Blanchard is far from sharing the enthusiasm of the ignorant crowd. With a coolness which few men have ever shown in a balloon, she tries to put out the fire. Not succeeding in this, she throws out all her ballast in order to moderate her descent. The unfortunate woman is seen looking down through space, trying to discover towards what point pitiless gravity is about to precipitate her.

Thanks to her presence of mind she will be saved, for the gas, driven back by the sudden increase of pressure, soon re-enters the interior of the balloon and extinguishes itself. There were then in the suburbs near where the balloon was, large gardens where an aeronaut might descend without danger. But the wind drives her on to the roof of a house against which her frail aerial bark strikes, and is overturned.

At the moment of shock, which is not violent,

The death of Madame Blanchard, July 7th, 1819

Madame Blanchard is heard to cry "A moi!" (Help!) But the last hour of the unfortunate daughter of the air has come. In gliding over the roof, her car encounters an iron cramp and is overturned. She does not expect so sudden a shock, and has not been holding on. When the people come up, the car and the balloon are still suspended on the roof, but Madame Blanchard, stretched on the pavement below, with broken shoulder and broken head, is breathing her last. °

The body was carried to the Tivoli Gardens, whereupon all music, dancing, and merrymaking suddenly ceased. The lights were put out, and the subdued crowds made their way home.

° From W. de Fonvielle, *Adventures in the Air* (London, 1877).

Long distance balloon voyage from London to Nassau, Germany, November 7–8th, 1836. The crew were Charles Green, pilot, Robert Hollond and Monck Mason

Chapter 6

Long-distance ballooning

Between 1820 and 1840, a major revolution took place in ballooning, led by a great British aeronaut, Charles Green, a fruit dealer's son who joined his father's business in the east end of London. By this time, William Murdock and Matthew Bolton had perfected a system of extracting gas from coal. It was used for lighting and domestic purposes, and gasworks had been established in a number of places in London and the provinces, with the usual apparatus of cylindrical gasholders which we see today. Coal gas was now readily and cheaply obtainable at any gasworks. It was this fact which led Charles Green and his followers to adopt coal gas for balloons instead of the lighter but more expensive hydrogen.

Green was a "man of the people" with few pretensions to education or scientific knowledge, though a good self-taught mechanic. It is said that he was led to experiment with coal gas for balloons after using it to light his father's shop. He learned ballooning the hard way, hitting trees and chimneys, being plunged into the sea off Brighton, and suffering other misfortunes. But he was a man of extraordinary character, tough, resolute, given to few words, with a powerful body and rosy face—in fact, as that authority on bal-looning Mr. L. T. C. Rolt happily puts it, "he could have sat as a model for the original John Bull."

Green made his first ascent in a coal-gas balloon from Green Park, London, on July 21st, 1821, the year of the coronation of George IV. It is not stated who financed the operation, but Green made a successful climb to 11,000 feet, coming to a rest about twelve miles north of London after the car had dragged along the ground for nearly a quarter of a mile. Just over a year after his first ascent he had one of the most alarming experiences of his career when, on August 1st, 1822, he made an ascent from Cheltenham in Glouchestershire, accompanied by a young reporter named Griffith, who represented the local newspaper, *The Cheltenham Chronicle.*

Heavy bets had been laid in London on how far Green would go, and then, as now, there were men who would commit any crime for money. Some malicious person or persons, taking advantage of the crowd which pressed around the car, half cut through the ropes which held it to the balloon. Green and his companion did not discover this until shortly after the ascent, when, one by one, three of the ropes broke. If the fourth had parted, the car would have plunged to the ground, but fortunately it held long enough for the two to climb up into the hoop below the balloon, to which was attached the mesh of ropes which held it prisoner. As the car was now hanging by one rope, all the ballast fell out, and the balloon soared rapidly to about 10,000 feet above the Cotswold Hills, with the two men hanging on desperately to the hoop.

Green could not reach the control line to open the

valve at the top of the balloon and release sufficient gas to effect a descent. As the balloon rose higher, it expanded, and there was imminent danger that it would burst. Then, one by one, the ropes forming the netting or mesh snapped with a noise like pistol shots; the balloon, completely out of control, began to bulge outwards through the holes caused by the breaking of the rope mesh.

But fortunately the gas began to leak, without asphyxiating the two aeronauts, and after a time the balloon began to descend, at first slowly and then with increasingly rapidity. The fields and woods below them rushed up at a frightening rate; people came out of their grey-stone cottages to see the horrifying sight; and at last, not far from Salperton, the balloon burst. Fortunately, it had by this time descended to within a few feet of the ground, and the two men were flung into a field in the parish of Notgrove. When the local people arrived on the scene, they found Green and his companion bruised and shaken, but otherwise unhurt.

Green, who was to make thousands of ascents, and of whom it has been said that he eventually reduced ballooning to a routine, never forgot that moment, even when he was a veteran of eighty. He always swore that criminals from London had severed the ropes, and it seems all too likely. One imagines that never again did the veteran balloonist begin an ascent without first examining the ropes.

Green did not make another ascent for a year after this near-catastrophe. Afterwards, year after year, he gave exhibitions of ballooning in many cities, but mainly in London. As time passed, he gradually acquired the well-deserved reputation of a great balloon pilot. He took thousands aloft on short journeys, and in order to compete with his rival showmen, he indulged in the usual tricks—fireworks displays, carrying a horse aloft, and so on. He also became a gifted constructor of balloons, and he introduced a number of interesting and useful innovations.

So much did his patrons trust and admire him that he was encouraged by the proprietors of the Vauxhall Pleasure Gardens in London to make a giant balloon at their expense. Two thousand yards of imported Italian raw silk were used. The gores were not sewn together after the old pattern, but cemented in place with a special adhesive invented by Green, which proved in the long run far more tenacious. The balloon was called the *Royal Vauxhall*. It had a capacity of 70,000 cubic feet and was as high as an average two-story building. Its extra volume was needed because coal gas has a lower lifting capacity than hydrogen. Even so, it is said, the balloon could lift no less than 4,982 pounds, and it required heavy weights and the combined efforts of some thirty-six policemen to hold it down prior to the ascent. Green also introduced a valuable device called the guide rope, a coil of rope over 1,000 feet in length, carried in the car, where it acted as ballast. When the balloon was at a certain height, the rope was paid out and trailed along the ground; the section which touched the ground relieved the *Royal Vauxhall* of the weight of that part. Over the sea, floats were used. The point of this invention was that the balloon could be maintained at a constant height. This, like the discharge of ballast, would cause the balloon, relieved of the weight, to ascend in a far more consistent and regular manner. By regulating the amount of rope paid out, Green could check the ascent or descent of the balloon. No one seems to have been concerned with the effect of the trailing rope on the land and property over which it passed.

Two English gentlemen, Monck Mason and Robert Hollond, were so impressed by the new balloon that they proposed to attempt a long-distance flight in the *Royal Vauxhall*, with Green as pilot. They offered to finance the flight themselves. Monck Mason was an artist, a flute-player, a lessee of Her Majesty's Theatre, and a patron of the opera; Hollond was a young Member of Parliament for Hastings. Green agreed to this venture, which was prepared with great care. In the balloon's car they carried provisions to last them three weeks: forty pounds of ham, beef, and tongue, forty-five pounds of fowls and preserves, forty pounds of sugar, bread, and biscuits, and two gallons each of sherry, port, and brandy, together with ingenious devices for making coffee by burning quicklime. Lamps attached to parachutes were to be used for signaling to those below.

Messrs. Guy and Hughes, owners of the balloon, sportingly allowed it to be used without any advance publicity. This was to be no ordinary balloon journey, but an odyssey.

The ascent was made at 1:30 p.m. on November 7th, 1836, under favourable northwesterly winds. The *Royal Vauxhall* soared over London and headed southward for Kent. The guide rope worked perfectly, the balloon maintaining a constant height from the ground. It rose when it encountered hills, and descended gently when the hills gave way to level plains. At twelve minutes to three, the aeronauts crossed the Medway and saw Rochester far below them. An hour later they were over

Canterbury, where a message was dropped by parachute for the Lord Mayor. It was nearly sunset when they sighted the sea, and as they passed over Dover Castle they distinctly heard the waves breaking on the shore.

Mason, Hollond, and Green then headed across the Channel at a steady pace, all Europe before them. Night was fast approaching; it became colder in the open car, and the aeronauts ate, drank, and toasted each other in port and brandy. "With many a joke touching the high flavour and exalted merits of the several viands," wrote Mason, "we contrived to do ample justice to the good cheer." * An hour after crossing Dover, they recognized the lights of Calais swimming out of the darkness far below them. They were dead on course. It had taken only one hour to cross the Channel, and their height was 3,000 feet. They lit a safety lamp and hung it above the car, and wrapped themselves snuggly in their warm clothing. The night lay ahead, with all its hazards and all its mystery.

The *Royal Vauxhall* sailed majestically on, underlit faintly by the lamp which hung above the car. Mason and Hollond tried to sleep, but Green kept constant watch as they flew silently over northern France and Belgium. Mason wrote afterwards:

> The scene itself was one which exceeds description. The whole plane of the Earth's surface, for many and many a league around, as far and farther than the eye could distinctly embrace, seems absolutely teeming with the fires of a watchful population, and exhibited a starry spectacle below, that almost rivalled in brilliancy the

* From Monck Mason, *Aeronautica* (London, 1848).

remote lustre of the concave firmament above. Incessantly, during the early part of the night, ere the vigilant inhabitants had finally retired to rest, large sources of light, signifying the presence of some more extensive community, would appear just looming above the distant horizon.*

Today, when night flying has become commonplace, one envies those three pioneers, who were seeing something which no men had ever seen before: Europe unfolding herself under the night sky. After a time, Green pointed to a fiery glow on the horizon, towards which they were heading. As they drew nearer, they saw the flame and smoke of furnaces. They consulted their maps and realized that they must be over Liège, in Belgium, with its iron and steel works. Then these too passed out of sight, and there was nothing ahead but blackness. Mason has a word about this too:

> An unfathomable abyss of darkness visible seemed to encompass us on every side; and as we looked forward into black obscurity in the direction in which we were proceeding, we could scarcely avoid the impression that we were cleaving our way through an interminable mass of black marble in which we were embedded, and which, solid though it seemed a few inches before us, seemed to soften as we approached it, in order to admit us still further within the precincts of its cold and dusky enclosure. Even the lights which at times we launched from the car, only tended to augment the intensity of the surrounding darkness.*

One can imagine Mason feverishly scribbling down his notes, determined to record his unique experience for posterity. But one also sees Green, the veteran aeronaut, looking anxiously ahead through the darkness, checking his guide rope and barometer, and waiting for the dawn to reveal a suitable landing place.

When at last the first pale light began to flush the horizon ahead, they were at the height of 12,000 feet, having crossed considerable mountains. It was bitterly cold, but, since they moved with the wind, they suffered its effects less than if they had been opposed to it. Below lay snowfields, and at first they thought they might be over Poland or even Russia. Soon they saw below them a region of wooded hills and fertile valleys. For some unexplained reason (they carried ample provisions for a longer flight) Green decided it was time to attempt a landing. He opened the valve, and the *Royal Vauxhall* began to descend.

The landing was not easy. Three times, owing to erratic winds, they threw out ballast and had to rise again; but eventually Green managed to bring the big balloon down near the edge of a wood which broke the force of the wind. When they climbed out, they found they were in Nassau, Germany, having travelled nearly five hundred miles in eighteen hours. At the nearby town of Weilburg they were handsomely entertained for several days; there were balls, concerts, and dinners in their honour, and at a special ceremony the *Royal Vauxhall* was rechristened *The Great Balloon of Nassau*, a name she retained for the rest of her long life.

Even greater feats of long-distance ballooning were attempted in the United States.

* *Ibid.*

After Blanchard made his first demonstration of balloon flight in America before George Washington in 1793, there had been a gradual growth of interest in ballooning in the newly created republic; indeed, experiments had been conducted in Philadelphia as early as 1784 under the patronage of Thomas Jefferson; and, as we have seen, it was an American, Dr. John Jeffries, who sponsored Blanchard's historic cross-Channel flight in 1785 and accompanied him on that perilous journey.

One well-known American aeronaut was Charles Ferson Durant, who made a number of spectacular ascents in the 1830s. The United States Army sought his advice when, in 1840, after nearly ten years of indecisive fighting against the Seminole Indians in Florida, Colonel John H. Sherburne suggested that balloons might be used to observe the movements of the elusive enemy. The Army's failure to bring the Seminole tribe to a decisive battle was due, Sherburne said, to the impossibility of locating them in thickly wooded country. If a balloon detachment was attached to each American column, and if these balloons ascended at night and noted the direction and position of the Indians' camp fires, it would be possible to send forces to surround and destroy the enemy in their encampments. Durant agreed to make an experimental balloon for nine hundred dollars, but nothing came of the offer. The War Department argued that, once the Indians realized they were being spied upon at night, they would light decoy fires where they would be least expected. The war came to an end three months later, without the assistance of military balloons.

Charles Durant, John La Mountain, John Wise, and Thaddeus Lowe constructed gigantic balloons—miniature airships, in fact—with which they made long and adventurous journeys. They faced hazards unknown to European balloonists, who could usually hope to descend in inhabited territory where they could obtain help. The American aeronauts, if carried far enough by the wind, might find themselves in sparsely populated or hostile territory, or they might be compelled to descend into one of the Great Lakes and drown. It is said that La Mountain, after a forced landing in Canada, in 1859, had to walk for four days without food or suitable clothing before he finally found the cabin of a Scottish settler.

In that same year a wealthy American balloon enthusiast named O. A. Gager financed an attempt at a transatlantic balloon flight—the first of several such attempts. The balloon, called the *Atlantic*, was a large aerostat containing 50,000 cubic feet of gas and was equipped with a lifeboat slung beneath the car, for use if the aeronauts had to come down on the ocean. Before attempting to cross the Atlantic, however, Wise and La Mountain, together with their patron, Gager, and a journalist, made a trial flight from St. Louis to the town of Henderson in Jefferson County, New York, covering 809 miles in just under twenty hours. This broke Green's record by some 300 miles, but it was still less than half the distance between Newfoundland and Ireland, and they could not be certain of obtaining favourable westerly winds throughout the journey. A terrifying moment over Lake Erie, when a storm forced them down almost to the water and they had to jettison the lifeboat to gain height, may have persuaded Wise, La Mountain, and their patron not to hazard their lives in a transatlantic crossing.

In theory, and given considerable luck, a giant balloon could have made the journey; and in that same year

Wise's rival Thaddeus Lowe determined to be the first to fly the Atlantic. He constructed a balloon of such size that even Wise's monster *Atlantic* was dwarfed by it. Lowe's balloon, called the *Great Western*, was 200 feet high and 130 feet wide and could lift twenty-two tons. Its envelope was made of 6,000 yards of fabric, and its wickerwork car was completely enclosed with canvas and provided with windows. Not only did it carry a lifeboat, but the boat was equipped with a steam engine which operated paddle wheels and a large airscrew, the angle of which could be adjusted in flight to provide forward propulsion or to assist in ascent or descent. It was the world's largest balloon, but, more than that, it was a rudimentary airship equipped with mechanical power. This was in 1859, more than half a century before the first German dirigibles flew.

But, alas, Lowe's monster came to grief on the 8th of September when, half an hour before lift-off, it was caught by a fierce squall and burst. Lowe, undeterred, made a new balloon and succeeded in flying from Cincinnati to Unionville (South Carolina) in nine hours, crossing the Appalachian Mountains en route. Unhappily he landed among hostile crowds and had to throw out ballast and take off rapidly. Not long afterwards he was forced to descend again, and again was threatened. He saved his life by threatening the mob with his revolver until at last a truce was declared and Lowe agreed to be taken to the nearby jail for interrogation. There he was recognized by a local hotel proprietor who had flown with him, and released. But his project of crossing the Atlantic had to be abandoned.

A daily newspaper, not long before, had prophesied a great future for ballooning:

Ballooning is evidently destined to become a marked feature of the age. Young America discarded steamboats long ago, and is becoming thoroughly disgusted with the annoyances and delays appurtenant to railroad travel. Let old fogies still drag along at the snail's pace of thirty miles an hour . . . let broad-shouldered rustics still patronise the iron horse . . . let who will wearily sail on the misty deep . . . but the coming year 1860 will witness another sight. . . . "Air Lines" of travel will exist otherwise than on handbills. . . . Distance will be annihilated and extension will cease to be one of the properties of matter. The Pacific Railroad question will no longer bother politicians. Through from New York to San Francisco in twenty-four hours. . . . Hurrah for Wise and La Mountain—for Bannister * and Balloons! †

This passage epitomized the lusty growth of Young America in the 1850s. The words were truly prophetic, for America *was* to have air lines spanning her vast distances, though with powered aircraft flying at far greater speeds than balloons. Yet the realization of the dream still lay rather far in the future. At the time we have reached, 1859–60, long-distance ballooning, including projects for crossing the Atlantic by air, was interrupted by the outbreak of the Civil War. It was not until 1919, exactly sixty years later, that the Atlantic was first flown —by two Englishmen, Alcock and Brown, flying a powered aircraft from west to east.

* W. D. Bannister of Michigan.
† *Detroit Daily Tribune,* July 25th, 1859.

Chapter 7

Balloons in the American Civil War

The Civil War (1861–65) brought military ballooning to the forefront again after the seventy years which had lapsed since balloons were used by the French Republican Army shortly after the Revolution.

The place of balloons in this bitterly heroic story is comparatively trivial and unimportant. But they do have this significance: In their clumsy, somewhat ludicrous way, they mark the incursion of modern science into the ancient art of warfare; and the fact that they were used to greater effect by the industrialized North than by the agricultural, slave-owning South, is in itself symbolic. Yet it must be admitted that the army of the North only blundered its way to the effective use of balloons, and the efforts of the pioneer American aeronauts, Allen, Wise, Lowe, and the rest, were frequently frustrated by the obtuseness and conservatism of the conventional military mind.

In the first year of the war the main centre of aeronautic activity was in the east, around Washington, D.C. General Robert E. Lee, commanding Virginia state forces, could have attacked Washington but refrained from doing so lest he be accused of aggression. The Union commander, the elderly General Winfield Scott, proposed to use his militia to defend the capital while training his newly recruited volunteers for a campaign in the autumn. But it was important for each side to gain control of the two railways which joined each other at Manassas Junction. In the spring of 1861, Washington, though not actively besieged, was aware of enemy forces uncomfortably close; the Confederate General P. G. T. Beauregard had gathered an army at Manassas Junction, thirty miles from the capital, and Harpers Ferry, a strategic position on another railway, had been taken by another Confederate force.

A demand grew in Washington that Beauregard's army be attacked and driven back. The general chosen to command this operation was Irvin McDowell, since Scott himself was too old to take the field.

It was during this period that the Union Army's first flirtation with ballooning took place. I say "flirtation" because, while the few well-known civilian aeronauts, Allen, La Mountain, Wise, and Lowe, were eager to offer their services, the military authorities, with one or two notable exceptions, were reluctant to use them. One of the exceptions was Captain Amiel W. Whipple, a young man who was among the few Union officers who realized the military potential of balloons for long-range observation. But even he had little knowledge of aerostatics or of the difficulties the civilian aeronauts would encounter when working under military conditions.

The first military aeronaut in the United States service was James Allen of Barrington, Rhode Island. He was the son of a sea captain, Sylvester Allen. When his father died, Allen, one of nine children, turned to any job which would help support his mother and family; he became in turn a cotton-mill hand, a farm labourer, and a merchant seaman, and then entered the printing trade. His interest in aerostatics began when he watched a bal-

loon ascent for the first time in Wilmington, Delaware.
Later, after reading all he could on the subject, he became friendly with the aeronaut Samuel A. King, of
Philadelphia, from whom he learned his craft. Allen
made his first solo ascent on July 4th, 1857, and later,
with King, gave exhibitions in nearly every state in New
England. Allen became so well known that he was often
called the New England Aeronaut; so, when the war
broke out in 1861, his advice was sought by the Union
Army. Unfortunately, like many pioneers, he suffered all
the disadvantages of being first in the field; the Army
authorities did not know how to use balloons properly,
and it took them a long time to learn.

Allen was a member of the Marine Corps of Artillery. He volunteered as an aeronaut and was attached
to General Burnside's First Rhode Island Regiment.
From the beginning his course was marked by mishaps
and disasters. One of his first difficulties was that his
generating equipment was inefficient and took a long
time to generate sufficient hydrogen to inflate a balloon
fully. The alternative was to fill it with coal gas from
a convenient gas main and then manoeuvre the inflated
balloon to the point at which the ascent was to be made.
This led to considerable trouble, as we shall see.

Allen made his first experimental ascent to 5,000 feet
on June 9th at Caton's farm, about a mile from the
capital, and this was judged a success. On the following
day, the First Rhode Island Regiment was ordered to
leave its camp at Washington and join the forces intended for an attack on Harpers Ferry. It is not certain,
but it seems possible, that Allen and his balloons went
along. Allen is said to have been ordered to make an
ascent in order to spy out the position of the Confederate
forces at the Ferry. But no attack was made, and Allen

returned to Washington, where his equipment underwent further tests.

These tests were highly unsuccessful. At the first attempt, when Captain Whipple ordered a subordinate, Lieutenant H. L. Abbot, to make a reconnaissance of the Confederate lines near Washington, Allen's generating equipment proved so ineffective that after a night's work the balloon was only half inflated. Nevertheless it was ordered aloft, with Abbot in the car. But a strong wind, which had sprung up during the night, tossed the half-inflated aerostat about to such an extent that the ground crew had difficulty in controlling it and poor Abbot, with his field glasses, found that accurate observation was impossible.

Despite this, the Union Army authorities still retained a curious interest in balloons. General McDowell was anxious to find out if balloons could be of any assistance in his forthcoming campaign against the Confederate Army in Virginia. Abbot, by this time had completely lost faith in Allen's hydrogen-generating apparatus, and recommended that for further tests the balloons should be inflated with coal gas at Alexandria and then taken, inflated, to the site of the ascent. This was the method which had been used, it will be remembered, by the French *aérostatiers* nearly seventy years earlier when moving an observation balloon from Maubeuge to Charleroi (see pages 68-69), although the French had not used coal gas.

But there was a difference. First, the American aeronauts themselves were civilians, and had no military status, nor were they trained in military ballooning. Second, the ground crews responsible for raising, lowering, and transporting Allen's balloons were a handful of soldiers drawn from any regiment which happened to be adjacent. They had no knowledge of balloons and were inexperienced in manoeuvring them on the ground. Third, though less important, the nineteenth century had introduced a new risk to the ground transport of inflated balloons—telegraph poles and overhead wires.

The result in this case was catastrophic. Allen's first balloon, an old civilian model made of cotton, was so worn that, on inflation from the gas main at Alexandria, it burst and shed its disintegrated remains on the ground crew. The second attempt appeared to be more successful. The balloon was inflated, again with coal gas, and then came the task of transporting it overland through difficult wooded country. The object was Falls Church, from which the aeronauts hoped to make a successful ascent and view the Confederate forces. But a strong breeze blew up, the huge envelope swayed and tossed in the wind, guide ropes became entangled, and the totally inexperienced soldiers holding the ropes were often nearly pulled off their feet. Lieutenant Abbot wrote: "We worried along, nearly to the point where our branch road diverged when suddenly a furious gust occurred. The detail, struggling and shouting, was slowly pulled towards the river in spite of their efforts, until the balloon in one of its stately plunges struck a telegraph pole. There was a puff of gas, and our work ended." *

It was not Allen's fault, but naturally, after this second disaster, the Union Army tended to lose interest in ballons, and he returned to Providence, Rhode Island, extremely chagrined. Later, when the Union Army Balloon Corps had been properly established under the supervision of another aeronaut, T. S. C. Lowe, Allen returned to render distinguished service.

* Quoted by F. Stansbury Haydon, *Aeronautics in the Union and Confederate Armies* (Baltimore, 1941).

Chapter 8

Thaddeus Lowe and John Wise

The higher echelons of the Union Army continued to regard balloons with a kind of love-hate. A few officers recognized that they could be of use, but the majority wished to have nothing to do with them, and this included the aging General Scott, commander-in-chief at the beginning of the war. Scott's attitude is well exemplified by his treatment of "Professor" Thaddeus Lowe, whose massive balloon the *Enterprise* loomed above the roofs of Washington at about the same time that Allen's was getting itself impaled on a telegraph pole, to the fury of Captain Whipple.

T. S. C. Lowe was a man of strong and engaging personality. He was born at Jefferson Mills, Coos County, New Hampshire, and was only twenty-nine when he arrived in Washington in the spring of 1861.

His progress as an aeronaut had been extremely rapid. He received only an ordinary grammar-school education, but his interest in science manifested itself early in his life. He was still a mere boy when he became interested in aerostatics and made his first experiments with kites, using the family cat as passenger. He built his first balloon in 1858 and made his first ascent from Ottawa.

A year later he intended to cross the Atlantic by

Civil War ballooning in the U.S.A. Lowe's balloon before the ascent at the battle of Fair Oaks, May 31st, 1862

balloon, utilizing the prevailing easterly air current. At Hoboken, New Jersey, he built a mammoth airship which he called the *City of New York*, but, as with many other pioneer aeronauts, his enterprise was dogged by misfortune, and the enormous craft was badly damaged.

In 1861 Lowe was one of several expert balloonists who were attempting to offer their services to the Union Army. He brought the *Enterprise* with him, but his trump card was a telegraphic system which, he claimed, would enable the observer in the car to transmit messages instantaneously to the ground by the Morse code. There were many at this time who seriously believed that, if telegraph wires were raised above the normal height of a telegraph pole and attached to a balloon flying at, say, 1,000 feet, atmospheric interference would interrupt or prevent the transmission of messages.

In Washington, Lowe had a very influential friend in Professor Joseph Henry, a noted physicist who was director of the Smithsonian Institution. Professor Henry enjoyed high status with political leaders, as did another of Lowe's backers, Murat Halstead, editor of the *Cincinnati Commercial*, who was friendly with Salmon P. Chase, secretary of the Treasury. Chase, of course, had the ear of President Lincoln himself.

On June 11th Lowe received an invitation to go at once to the White House. Lincoln was friendly and interested in all that Lowe had to tell him about the military advantages of the observation balloon, and later the War Department apportioned Lowe a small sum of money to enable him to carry out his experiments. On June 18th the *Enterprise*, inflated with 20,000 cubic feet of coal gas, rose above the grounds of the Columbian Armoury, adorned with two large American flags and a Union Jack.

In the car, besides Lowe, were Superintendent Burns of the Washington Telegraph Company and a telegraph operator named Robinson, whose pocket transmitter was attached to the end of half a mile of fine insulated wire. The other end of the wire was attached to a land line between the ground station and the Alexandria office of the telegraph company. As the mooring ropes were paid out, the *Enterprise* rose to a height of about five hundred feet. Then Robinson, at Lowe's dictation, tapped out the following message to President Lincoln, the first ever to be telegraphed from the air:

TO THE PRESIDENT OF
THE UNITED STATES

Sir:

This point of observation commands an area nearly fifty miles in diameter. The city, with its girdle of encampments, presents a superb scene. I have pleasure in sending you the first despatch ever telegraphed from an aerial station, and in acknowledging indebtedness for your encouragement for the opportunity of demonstrating the availability of aeronautics in the military service of the country.

Lincoln is said to have telegraphed a reply to Lowe's greeting, but there is no record of it. Then the *Enterprise* was hauled down and, still inflated, drawn through the streets on a wagon to the grounds of the White House, from which Lincoln watched the operation through an upper window. On the following afternoon more ascents were made from the lawns of the White House, and again the telegraph was demonstrated. There were numerous spectators, including Captain Whipple. Whipple and his superior officer, Major Hartman Bache, were already in contact with another aeronaut, John Wise, and it may well have been the success of Lowe's demonstration that persuaded them to commission Wise to make a balloon more suitable for military use.

One of General McDowell's brigade commanders had reported from "a reliable source" that some 20,000 Confederate troops were massing between Manassas and Fairfax Court House; but he had no means of confirming the enemy's position. McDowell immediately thought of Lowe and his balloon. He ordered Captain Whipple to telegraph his superior, Major Bache of the Topographical Bureau, asking him to obtain Lowe's services immediately. It never seems to have occurred to either of them that Lowe, as a civilian, was not subject to military orders. Nevertheless the aeronaut made immediate preparations to take his balloon to Arlington to make observations.

The *Enterprise* arrived at Arlington on June 22nd, and

Lowe immediately made an ascent but did not report anything of interest. Next morning, at 4:00 a.m., the balloon party was ordered forward to Falls Church. There were further delays on the way, when Union guards told the aeronaut that the ground through which he was to advance was not held by their troops, and warned him to keep a keen watch for enemy formations. Lowe ordered the *Enterprise* to be winched up so that he could keep a look-out. Whipple telegraphed his headquarters, asking, "Do you know what prevents the ascension?" and pointing out that visibility would soon decrease owing to inclement weather.

When at last Lowe and his party did arrive at Falls Church after an exhausting journey, Whipple allowed them a rest before the ascent. When the big balloon finally rose, visibility was so bad, and the winds were so strong, that no observation of any importance could be made. At six o'clock Lowe again went aloft, accompanied by Captain Whipple. They could not even distinguish the village of Fairfax Court House through their glasses, though it was only eight miles away. But large clouds of dust observed in that direction might, they thought, be caused by substantial bodies of cavalry. On June 24th Major Leonard Colburn made the ascent and produced a detailed map of the surrounding country which won the praise of his chief, Brigadier General Tyler.

Lowe received some guarded praise from the military authorities, but some sections of the press were sardonic. One journalist wrote:

> Professor Lowe would fain get high
> At Government expense;
> With big balloon he'd scale the moon

To spy Virginia's fence;
To spot the camps of rebel scamps
With Telegraph and glass—
You ask me, friend, how this will end?
And I reply—in gas!

Lowe returned to Washington on June 25th to discover that John Wise had submitted a very low estimate for a military balloon which it was suggested Lowe might operate. Lowe was not having any of this and firmly declined.

We have already briefly met John Wise; it was he who, with companions, flew from St. Louis to Henderson, New York, a distance of over 800 miles, in under twenty hours. He was already fifty-one, with twenty-six years of ballooning behind him, when he volunteered for service in the Union Army, not at first as an aeronaut, but as a cavalry captain. He came from Lancaster, Pennsylvania, and personally raised a regiment of volunteers from that town with the idea of leading it in battle.

But the Army had other plans for Wise. While he was waiting for his offer to be accepted, the Bureau of Topographic Engineers called him for service as a balloonist. Major Bache had telegraphed Wise, asking how much a balloon capable of lifting five hundred pounds would cost and how much the aeronaut would demand for operating it. Wise replied that he would construct such a balloon for $300 and fly it himself at no cost to the army. But Whipple, Bache's subordinate, was not satisfied, having had the bitter experience of Allen's efforts and having also seen the giant balloon *Enterprise* constructed by "Professor" Thaddeus Lowe, complete with telegraph.

So, after a lapse of some days, Wise received a second telegram, this time asking for an estimate for a more elaborate balloon "constructed of best India raw silk, capacity 20,000 cubic feet, cordage of linen etc." Wise replied as promptly as before, giving an estimate of $850, which was accepted.

This, the first true military balloon made in the United States, had several novel features. The floor of the car was fitted with thick armour plate to protect the aeronauts from musket fire at short range. Wise had also considered what might happen if enemy troops overran the launching station and captured the mooring ropes. To provide against such an emergency, he stored within the car small bombs and percussion grenades, which he proposed to rain down upon the enemy troops and so induce them to let go the ropes. Failing this, he had incorporated a device below the car by which the ropes could be cut and the balloon freed. He hoped that favouring winds would then float him into friendly territory.

It was all very ingenious and well thought out—with one exception: there was no provision for inflating the balloon on the site with transportable generating equipment. It had to be filled with coal gas from a convenient main, and then manhandled to the point from which it was to ascend. And handled, not by men experienced in the task, but by soldiers detailed for the job from whichever unit happened to be handy.

We must now return to the war, and especially to General McDowell's assault force, which marched out of Washington with infantry, cavalry, and artillery, intent on meeting the enemy, prying loose his hold on part of the Shenandoah Valley with its vital railway, and possibly advancing on Richmond, the Confederate

John Wise

capital. "Forward to Richmond!" was the exultant cry of the Washington press. Captain Whipple was already in position in McDowell's advance lines and was eagerly expecting Wise's arrival with his balloon. He had, in fact, telegraphed the day before that he needed the balloon with the forward troops of the advancing army for reconnaissance and observation.

Wise was assisted by twenty picked men from the 26th Pennsylvania Infantry; Captain Theodore Talbot directed that a wagon and team be placed at the balloon party's disposal, and a Major Myer took command of the enterprise. Unhappily, there were frustrating delays, and the unit did not take up their line of march from the Columbian Armoury (where the balloon had been inflated) until July 21st, although the original plan had been that Wise would leave on the 19th, and on the

109

20th make his ascent from a point two miles from the Confederate lines, carrying with him an officer who was to observe enemy movements.

That delay of thirty hours was fatal.

> The inflated balloon was towed by the detail, who held the mooring ropes in their hands and manoeuvred the swaying envelope past telegraph poles and wires that lined the way. Fortunately a bright moon, unobscured by clouds, gave light to help them on their task. . . . Grey dawn was breaking when the unit passed through Georgetown. Progress after leaving the city was even more difficult. The long Georgetown aqueduct bridge had to be crossed, after which the line of march followed the Chesapeake and Ohio Canal. More than once the men had to wade and swim the canal in order to tow the balloon around projecting trees and thick clumps of tall bushes. °

Later the road wound through woodland, and the mooring ropes had to be delicately manoeuvred to prevent their becoming entangled in the branches. By noon of Sunday—that fateful Sunday, July 21st—the party was only halfway to the scene of battle. But the ominous sound of conflict came beating back at them through the trees; in the distance, above the forest, a thick smoky pall rose into the sky. There was the continual, battering thunder of heavy guns, mixed with the harsh, stuttering crash of sustained musket fire.

The battle of Bull Run was reaching its climax, and, unknown to the struggling balloon party, General Mc-

° From F. Stansbury Haydon, *Aeronautics in the Union and Confederate Armies* (Baltimore, 1941).

Dowell's gallant force was wavering towards a retreat. Captain Whipple, at his observation post near the front line, waited impatiently for the slow, cumbersome advance of the clumsy aerostat and its sweating escort. Major Myer, who commanded it, urged the party on, and they made every effort to increase their pace as they came nearer to the acrid smell of gunsmoke and the roar of battle.

But still Myer was not satisfied. Overruling Wise, he ordered that the balloon be mounted on the horse-drawn wagon. The horses were urged to a fast trot, the balloon dipping and swaying above, often scraping the trees. When the wagon was driven through a narrow passage between the trees, near the town of Fairfax, the worst happened. The balloon was jammed in the thick upper foliage, and frantic efforts failed to release it. Myer, inflamed by the sounds of battle, ordered that the horses be spurred to a gallop in the hope that this would free the balloon without damage. There was a terrible rending sound as the envelope tore open, then the hiss of escaping gas; and slowly the huge envelope emptied, draping its empty carcass over the trees, over the wagon, and on the forest track. It is not related whether or not Wise said, "I told you so."

All we know is that Wise was ordered to transport the torn balloon back to Washington, while Myer spurred his horse towards the battlefield. He served with gallantry in what remained of the action, and General McDowell mentioned him in his dispatches. But the battle of Bull Run was virtually over, and for days afterwards refugees from McDowell's shattered army streamed back to Washington. The South had won the first great battle of the Civil War.

Chapter 9

Captive versus
free-flying balloons

After this debacle Wise fell out of favour, and he returned to Lancaster, Pennsylvania, a disappointed man. His health broke down, and he retired from active duty to write about military aeronautics. Lowe, a much younger man, had already gained the favour of President Lincoln, but his progress was hindered at first by the recalcitrant attitude of the commander-in-chief of the Union forces, General Scott. After trying four times to get an interview with the general, Lowe again presented himself to Lincoln. The President put on his old battered stovepipe hat, said "Come on," and walked with Lowe to Scott's headquarters. This time the guard turned out to welcome the President, and both, of course, were admitted. Scott offered Lowe a civilian post at thirty dollars a day whenever he made an ascent, payment for the gas, and a ground crew of twenty men. This did not suit the aeronaut, who was aiming at higher things. What he really wanted was a permanent post and the authorization to make a balloon of special construction at the Army's expense.

He got in touch with his friend Professor Henry of the Smithsonian Institution who used his influence to persuade the Army to make a balloon "better adapted for the purpose." Though Lowe was recognized as a military aeronaut, his troubles were by no means over, for another rival had appeared—the gallant free-lance balloonist John La Mountain, who, having entered the service by a different route, was eager to demonstrate the technique of free ballooning for aerial reconnaissance, a method of which Lowe strenuously disapproved. But that method was to prove, for a time, extremely effective.

The romantically named John La Mountain was born about 1830—his birth date has not been established —and would have been roughly of the same age as Thaddeus Lowe—about thirty-one—when he sought to serve the Union as an aeronaut. Like Allen, he had been a seaman; but, apart from his epic flight with Gager and Wise in 1859, not much is known about his early career. He was a more flamboyant character than either Wise or Lowe—an adventurer, possessed of great courage and rare physical strength. He was less scientific-minded than Wise and far less of a politician than Lowe. But he had the romantic charm which often accompanies erratic personalities. Lowe detested him, and the feeling was reciprocated.

After the usual unavailing attempts to interest the Army authorities in Washington—none of his letters were even acknowledged—La Mountain was lucky enough to attract the attention of Major General Benjamin F. Butler, then in charge of Fortress Monroe, from which he commanded the Department of Virginia. This was in early July. Butler wrote to La Mountain offering him employment as an aerial observer.

The Major General's military problems could be summed up as follows: The possession of Fortress Monroe gave him the opportunity of blockading the Confederate capital of Richmond and even of launching an attack on it if given a preponderance of force. On the other hand, the fortress was cut off by the York and James rivers, which were accessible to Confederate warships. And opposite the fortress, at a place called Sewall's Point, the enemy had built gun emplacements, and troops were reported in considerable force in this area.

Butler was hampered by insufficient intelligence of the Confederate forces ranged against him; this is why he needed La Mountain and his two balloons. The flat country was ideal for aerial surveillance, and if necessary the aerostats could be flown from ships, which could be moved from place to place. La Mountain arrived with his smaller balloon and made a successful ascent on July 31st, ten days after the battle of Bull Run. What he saw greatly reassured Major General Butler. For a distance of thirty miles no unusual activity could be observed.

Throughout the first half of August, La Mountain continued to make ascents, several times from ships. These little ships, the armed transport *Fanny* and the tug *Adriatic*, were therefore the world's first aircraft carriers. The *Fanny* steamed to a place opposite Sewall's Point, and from 2,000 feet La Mountain reported the building of additional fortifications, with embrasures and gun pits. But, once he had expended all his gas, La Mountain was in a quandary; he asked permission to leave and bring back his larger balloon, the *Saratoga*, together with a water-decomposition gas generator, which, he said, would do away with the need for sulphuric acid and scrap iron. He also had grandiose ideas of bombing from the air and of making free flights over enemy positions.

Butler authorized him to go, but, while he was away, Butler was moved to another command. When La Mountain returned, he found that he was under a new commander, General J. E. Wool, who knew nothing about him, Butler having left no instructions. As Wool seemed undecided what to do, La Mountain made his way to Washington with the *Saratoga*, hoping to obtain employment with the Union Army there.

By this time Thaddeus Lowe, after his initial failures, had established himself firmly with the Army, especially with Generals George B. McClellan and Fitz-John Porter. Lowe naturally did not relish the idea of La Mountain treading on what he regarded as his territory, especially as the two had been rivals and La Mountain had made some very injudicious remarks about Lowe's telegraphic system. Also they were temperamental opposites.

Lowe was convinced that the only way to use balloons for military observation was to moor them and then, from moderate heights, telegraph information to the ground. He also had the grand conception of a balloon corps with a number of aeronauts operating from certain positions under his command, then moving quickly as the line of battle changed. La Mountain, while admitting the value of the captive balloon, which he had used with considerable success already, was fired by the idea of free flights: allowing himself to be carried by the east wind over the enemy lines, then throwing out ballast, rising to a greater height, and being carried back into friendly territory by the prevailing west winds blowing at higher altitudes.

There were a number of obvious snags in such a method. First, La Mountain could not be certain of being able to land in the same place from which he took off. Second, he might be forced to land behind the enemy lines. Third, in free flight he had no means of sending immediate information to the ground, and long delays might ensue before he could get his information back to headquarters. Fourth, in order to land, he would have to release gas; how was his balloon to be reinflated quickly if he landed at some distance from his starting point?

Despite all these objections, La Mountain was enthusiastic about his scheme, which did have certain definite advantages, the main one being that in free flight he would be directly over the enemy positions and able to observe them more clearly than from a captive balloon. General McClellan was impressed by this fact and wished to encourage La Mountain, as did General Porter. La Mountain was officially attached to the Army of the Potomac, much to the annoyance of Lowe.

McClellan, realizing quite early that this rivalry existed, instructed Porter to summon the two aeronauts to his tent and metaphorically knock their heads together. Porter pointed out to them that, although they were working in the same area, there was no reason why they should not both work for the common cause, Lowe with his captive balloons and La Mountain with his free flights. But the two young men, each in his early thirties, remained suspicious of each other.

At first, however, all went well. John La Mountain made a number of daring flights over the Confederate lines in his free balloon, some of which yielded valuable military information. His courage and skill were remarkable—courage since he had no military status and could have been shot as a spy if forced to descend in Confederate territory, skill since, though he was at the mercy of the winds, he somehow always managed to land in or near the right place.

On October 18th, after some experimental ascents, La Mountain launched out over the Confederate lines in the *Saratoga* and was blown steadily westwards. From between 1,000 and 2,000 feet he made a number of careful observations. He noted a heavy-gun battery at Aquia Creek and, half a mile to the rear of this position, tented accommodation for about 1,200 men. He noted a large enemy force moving in several directions. The remarkable fact is that he was able to make these correct observations without military training. Then he hurled out his ballast, rose to a much greater height, caught the west wind, and flew back over Union territory, landing in the camp of Brigadier General Louis Blenker's German Brigade.

Again and again the young aeronaut rose into the air, cast off his mooring ropes, and allowed himself to be carried far over Confederate territory. Oddly enough, he never took photographs, which would have been technically feasible at this period. In fact, a Captain Albert Tracey had written to General Butler:

> Why not . . . obtain, at a moment in the air, a picture of the country beneath, with the camps, batteries, and perhaps well-defined impressions of any body of troops . . . of the enemy? Fine stereoscopic glasses would reveal to the eye with the strongest individuality each and every object upon the plates. Of course pictures might be

multiplied *ad infinitum* by the usual process, and
as many copies furnished in as many directions
as desirable. Thus we might come to possess information of the most reliable character of the
position and operations of the enemy. *

But there is no evidence that La Mountain ever carried
a camera with him, either under Butler or under Mc-
Clellan. Thus a great opportunity was lost.

On one occasion a war correspondent flew with La
Mountain. He left us an account of his experience, from
which the following is an extract:

Stepping into the car with him, he cut loose,
and in a moment, as it were, our army lay beneath
us, a sight well worth a soul to see—brown earth
fortifications, white tented encampments, and
black lines and squares of solid soldiery in every
direction. So enchanted was I with the scene that
I well-nigh forgot that we were drifting enemy-
ward, until Fairfax Court House lay beneath us,
and I had my first sight of the enemy, in the
roaming squads of rebel cavalry visible in that
vicinity. Soon Centreville and Manassas came in
sight, and there in their bough huts lay the great
Army of the South. All along they stretched south-
easterly towards the Potomac, on whose banks
their batteries were distinctly visible. So plain
were they below, their numbers could be noted
so carefully that not a regiment could escape the
count. . . . The Professor [La Mountain], satisfied

* Captain Albert Tracey (10th U.S. Infantry) to Butler, June 16th,
1861 (Butler papers).

with his reconnaissance . . . after noting down the strength of the forces and their position, discharged ballast and started for that higher current to bring him back. Now I acknowledge I looked anxiously and nervously for a backward movement, conscious that to come down where we were was death. . . . Up, up, up, we went, but still bearing west and south. I looked at the Professor's face. It was calm and confident, so I felt assured that all was right. That assurance became a settled thing when in a few moments we commenced passing gently back to the east. We had struck the Professor's current. Back, back we went, as though a magnet drew us, until our own glorious stars and stripes floated beneath us, and we came down gradually and smoothly into the encampments of General Franklin's division. *

"C'est magnifique, mais ce n'est pas la guerre," as someone remarked of another war. For the fact was that La Mountain's efforts—though daring, dramatic, and at times fruitful in their results—were far less useful from the military viewpoint than the farseeing, systematic work of Lowe. By the winter of 1861 Lowe had established himself so firmly with the Union Army that he had been empowered to order several balloons especially built at the Army's expense and was recruiting aeronauts and ground crews to man them.

In December 1861 two of Lowe's military balloons were idle in Washington, awaiting transport to appro-

---

* Frank (war correspondent) to the editor of the *Boston Journal*, November 16th, 1861.

119

priate launching points, when La Mountain had the misfortune to lose the *Saratoga*, which, owing to mishandling by the inexperienced ground crew, had broken away in a strong wind and floated off over the enemy lines, never to be seen again. La Mountain was then left with his older balloon, the *Atlantic*, which was badly worn and in need of repair. Somewhat naturally he wanted to get his hands on one of Lowe's Army balloons, and he sent a message to General W. B. Franklin asking for permission to use one.

While permission was being sought, La Mountain continued his operations with the old *Atlantic*. The fabric easily crumbled and tended to leak, but this did not deter La Mountain. On December 10th he soared over the Confederate territory and made "one of the most detailed inspections of the enemy positions that he had yet made. Hovering for several hours over hostile lines, he noted many items of importance and then rose to an altitude of 17,000 feet, entering the prevailing easterly current, and descended in the camp of the 2nd Rhode Island Volunteer Infantry, four miles from the capital." *

The skill and courage needed for this enterprise in an old, worn balloon, particularly in descending, after a long flight at high altitude, into a military camp within a short distance from headquarters, needs no emphasis. This and other flights by La Mountain annoyed the Confederate army: General Beauregard, incensed with the Union forces for "floating their infernal balloon over our heads," gave orders for deceptive installations: dummy artillery made of blackened logs and stovepipes was set

* From F. Stansbury Haydon, *Aeronautics in the Union and Confederate Armies* (Baltimore, 1941).

up in positions where it would be observed. There is no record that any aeronaut was fooled by these.

The bitter rivalry between Lowe and La Mountain continued as was inevitable when the press, praising the efforts of the free-lance aeronaut, suggested that they would soon "eclipse those of his rival Professor Lowe."

The crunch was not long in coming. In February 1862, weeks after he had sent his original request to General Franklin, La Mountain approached Colonel Macomb, who was then supervisor of the balloon service, asking for one of Lowe's balloons. But Lowe, in the intervening period, had entrenched himself. He had carried on a "paper war" against La Mountain, sending to General McClellan some of the more irritating press clippings comparing La Mountain's daring exploits with his own comparatively mundane work, and so ingratiating himself with McClellan that the latter had the following message sent to La Mountain: "It is his [General McClellan's] wish that all balloons shall be under the superintendence of Mr. Lowe. Upon this basis, if you can come to an understanding with Mr. Lowe, it may be of interest to yourself and the service." One can imagine La Mountain's reaction. It would be as easy to ask General Beauregard to cooperate with General McClellan as to expect La Mountain to throw in his lot with his rival.

This was the atmosphere in which the two met in February, when La Mountain sought to obtain one of Lowe's balloons. Lowe refused and eventually wrote to McClellan's headquarters a venomous letter in which he said that La Mountain was "a man who is known to be unscrupulous, and prompted by jealousy or some other motive, has assailed me without cause through the press and otherwise for several years. . . . He has tampered with my men, tending to a demoralisation of them, and in short he has stopped at nothing to injure me . . . so much so that it is impossible for me to have any contact with him, as an equal in my profession, with any self-respect." *

In the end Lowe won, of course. He had been the first aeronaut to make a success of balloon operations with the Union Army. The high and gilded staff, weary of the dissensions of these two prima donnas, bore this in mind when deciding who should be sacrificed. It was, naturally, La Mountain, who was dismissed from the service on February 19th, 1862. He returned to his home, and that is practically the last we hear of him.

Lowe eventually received the title Chief Aeronaut with the Union Army—though he remained a civilian, as did all the aeronauts whom he recruited to serve under him. These men were a mixed bunch. Among them were James Allen, John B. Starkweather, Ebenezer Mason, John R. Dickinson, and Ebenezer Seaver. The last invented for himself a uniform which aroused the derision of Lowe's father, Clovis Lowe, who served for a time with the corps. Lowe senior wrote: "General Sickles could not have put on so many things or so many shoulder straps as he [Seaver] did."

On the whole, Lowe was well served by his staff, though one or two, as in any modern air squadron, were a little wild. It must be realized that the professional balloonists of this time were usually showmen, and perhaps it was this which made them paint their balloons in gaudy colours displaying patriotic symbols—as, for instance, the face of George Washington—and even to

* The Lowe papers, quoted by Haydon, *op. cit.*

American Civil War. The Union balloon *Intrepid*

decorate the cars beneath the balloons with a sprinkling
of white stars on a sky-blue ground. The sight of these
garish monsters hovering over the battle lines must
have provided considerable encouragement to the Union
troops and annoyance to their enemies.

Nevertheless, despite these interludes of showmanship, the abiding impression with which one is left is
that of Thaddeus Sobieski Constantine Lowe—serious,
concerned, and slightly aloof on his horse, wearing semi-
military dress (trousers stuffed into high riding boots,

a long dark coat with military frog fasteners, and a black slouch hat), riding from post to post examining his men's equipment, registering their complaints—constantly supervising an enterprise which, though abortive, was in reality the precursor of the United States Air Force. Few details escaped him. Each balloon unit was equipped not only with its aerostat but with a complete kit of spare parts and a portable gas generator drawn by a four-horse wagon.

Lowe also saw to it that each unit was provided with the raw materials for gas production; sulphuric acid in carboys and masses of iron filings, to be used in his specially designed portable gas generators. Operations at sea also came within his scope. He supervised the adaptation of a ship, the *G. W. Parke Curtis*, which operated from the Potomac and was altered ingeniously for the accommodation and flying of observation balloons.

Despite all his frustrations and difficulties, Lowe managed to organize and maintain his Balloon Corps from 1861 to 1863, becoming more and more professional as his experience increased. Wherever the Union Army moved, there the Balloon Corps moved also, observing enemy encampments from altitudes between 500 and 5,000 feet, watching, with powerful field glasses, the troops and tents, the artillery batteries and emplacements, and sometimes the smoke of battle. Information was passed to the ground by telegraph, by flags, or by other signals. Often the balloons were shot at, the enemy gunners becoming more and more expert as the war continued. Yet the aeronauts still leaped into their cars, cast off, and rose into the sky amid the crack and thunder of Confederate guns.

To sum up in the words of Haydon:

> They accompanied the army through the sloughs and mudholes of the Peninsula's impossible roads; through the mire and snow from Washington to the slaughter-field of Fredericksburg in mid-winter; over the mountain roads of Western Virginia after Antietam; and over the wagon tracks of the Wilderness in the Chancellorsville campaign. Only once, during the critical action of the Seven Days when McClellan withdrew to James River, was it necessary to abandon any of this equipment to the enemy. *

* F. Stansbury Haydon, *op. cit.*

The Franco-Prussian War 1870–71. Building balloons in the Orléans Station, Paris

Chapter 10

The siege of Paris

The use of balloons in warfare in the nineteenth century was not limited to the American Civil War. Bombing from balloons had been tried by the Austrians during their siege of Venice in 1849, but most of the balloons— each fitted with a 24-pound bomb and a fuse—fell into their own lines, and those which reached the city did only trivial damage. The air currents were too unpredictable to make bombing practical.

The most extraordinary use of free balloons was during the Prussian siege of Paris in 1870–71. The city was totally encircled by the Prussian troops. All railways and roads were blocked, and penetration of the enemy lines was impossible.

The idea of using balloons for communicating with the rest of France, particularly with the provisional government at Tours, came not from the military authorities but from certain French aeronauts. On the morning of September 23rd the Prussians were astonished to see a large balloon rocketing up from the besieged city; before they could level their guns at it, it was out of range. The aeronaut, Jules Duruof, flying an old, leaking balloon, deliberately chose this method of making his ascent, throwing out ballast rapidly in order to escape enemy gunfire. He landed safely three hours and fifteen minutes later six kilometers from Evreux, well behind the Prussian lines, with his 227 pounds of mail, which was then sent to Tours. It is said that Duruof enraged the Prussians by dropping visiting cards on their lines as he flew overhead.

After this initial success, balloons were used more and more to carry mail and emissaries out of Paris, usually with complete success. The problem of sending mail into the city was solved by the use of carrier pigeons—supplied, at first, by a pigeon-fancier named Van Roosebeke. Each balloonist took with him a number of pigeons, which returned to Paris with answers to the mail sent out of the city. Sometimes as many as thirty-four pigeons were carried in a single balloon.

The supply of private balloons soon gave out since they could not be returned to the capital. Besides *Le Neptune*, in which Duruof made his spectacular ascent on September 23rd, there was *La Ville de Florence*, which left two days later carrying 231 pounds of mail and three pigeons. On the 29th a famous aeronaut named Louis Godard took off in a strange contraption consisting of two small balloons, named *Hirondelle* and *Napoléon*, connected by a pole. Godard was in the car of the *Hirondelle*, and a passenger was carried in the other car. The whole construction, renamed *Les Etats-Unis*, landed safely near Mantes. Still later the last of the private balloons, called *La Céleste*, piloted by another well-known aeronaut, Gaston Tissandier, ascended on the last day of September, 1870.

By this time the authorities, realizing that the balloon postal system *did* work, made preparations to manufacture large numbers of balloons to maintain the service. As manufacturing centres they chose two of the main railway stations of Paris, the Gare du Nord and the Gare d'Orléans. People, mainly women, were recruited by the hundreds to make the balloons, which, being intended only for one journey, were made of cheap, expendable material—calico. The station platforms were scenes of intense activity. Great bales of balloon cloth were hung up to dry from the columns supporting the station roofs. Hundreds of women were to be seen cutting the cloth and sewing it together, by hand or with sewing machines. In other parts of the stations the completed balloons, after varnishing, were inflated with air to test for leaks. Finally the balloons, inflated with coal gas, ascended from one or the other of these railways stations, usually gaily coloured (for this, after all, was France) and piloted by sailors. The supply of experienced aeronauts having been almost exhausted, it was necessary to use inexperienced amateurs, who, after a very brief instruction in the art of ballooning, did remarkable service. And all carried pigeons; in some cases the pigeon-fanciers themselves, mainly working-men, went aloft with their birds.

It was typical of the Parisians that not only did they paint their balloons in bright colours, as if to mock the encircling Prussians, but they gave each a name, usually that of some famous person; there were the *Montgolfier*, the *George Sand*, the *Volta*, the *Newton*, and the *Jacquard*.

Wildfrid de Fonvielle, a contemporary observer and a distinguished aeronaut, wrote:

A uniform model was adopted for postal balloons, economical, comparatively substantial, and rather elegant. They had a capacity of 72,000 cubic feet. Including those which were found at the time of the capitulation of Paris, between seventy and eighty were manufactured at a cost of about £160 each. The number of letters carried

129

having exceeded three millions, the postal re-
ceipts were increased by more than £36,000. . . .
One can easily believe that the wonderful spectacle of these ascents will never be forgotten.*

One sophisticated refinement of the balloon postal
service may surprise those who imagine that the use of
microfilm for photographing documents is a modern
development. It was known and used during the siege
of Paris almost exactly one hundred years ago, and the
motive behind its invention was the need to fasten a
large amount of mail to a carrier pigeon. Since there
was a strict limit to the weight these birds could carry,
the photographic experts got to work. One photographer
"devised a method of copying two or three hundred
despatches on a square of paper which could be fastened
under the wing of a pigeon. A powerful glass or micro-
scope was used to decipher the messages." †

The ultimate refinement came, however, when a
photographer named Dagron produced tiny films, coated
with collodion, which could be magnified to practically
any extent. When a carrier arrived in Paris with one
of these films attached to its leg, the film was taken to
a hall in the Rue de Grenelle, where a "magic lantern"
(the Victorian ancestor of the modern slide projector)
threw an enlarged image of the letters onto a screen,
from which they were copied by clerks.

One might ask how a reliable postal service could be
based on such an uncertain mode of communication.
The answer is that the messages were duplicated: fifteen
birds would each carry the same film, and one of these
was reasonably sure to reach the city and be found.

* W. de Fonvielle, *Adventures in the Air* (London, 1877).
† *Ibid.*

The Franco-Prussian War. A narrow escape for a balloon leaving Paris

De Fonvielle calculated that each pigeon could carry five thousand dispatches, containing matter equal to thirty-six pages, all recorded on six collodion-coated films. This seems an exaggeration, but he was writing at the time, and one can only take his word for it.

One of the outstanding exploits of the siege was the escape from Paris of Leon Gambetta, brilliant lawyer and statesman who headed the French resistance to the Prussians. Named Minister of the Interior by the provisional government of national defence when Napoleon III capitulated to the Germans, he planned to fly out of the beleaguered city to arouse the provinces. Hoping to equip fresh armies from areas beyond the reach of the enemy troops, he left Paris on October 7, 1870, in a balloon and floated over the German lines to Amiens. There he assumed direction of the government of unoccupied France and prepared to wage guerrilla warfare against the invaders.

Not all the balloons flown from Paris in 1870 flew beyond the enemy lines, or escaped disaster. There was the *Galilée*, which fell into Prussian hands. The *Niepce*, pierced by enemy musketballs, fell within enemy territory, but the photographer, aided by the inhabitants of the district in which the aerostat fell, was able to escape and send back some of the carrier pigeons with films containing fresh news, including that of his escape.

Here is a description by de Fonvielle which conveys a vivid idea of what it was like to escape from beleaguered Paris in a balloon:

I gave the order to let go the craft. The order was complied with, with extraordinary precision, and we ascended gently, travelling to the northern part of the city. An immense crowd had collected round the gasworks; the streets were paved with hats, and tremendous shouts answered our cry, "Long live the Republic! Down with the German butchers!" It was like the voice of the earth coming to the heavens; our golden ball lifted itself towards Olympus' gates, loaded with human prayers. . . .

. . . We soon arrived at the gates of Paris, and we saw desolated fields, disappearing one after another. I recognized different parts of this once happy land, where I had wandered during so many happy years. I was looking at a certain spot when the first shot was heard by my distracted ear. I laughed merrily, because the barometer showed more than 5,000 feet, and I told my passengers: "This is the beginning of German music, which is played down below by a full German band. Herr von Bismarck [the German Chancellor] reproached our dear Trochu [a French general] for wasting his powder, when shelling the German works. I wonder if the German powder, even with the skill of Mein Herr Krupp, is better employed in shelling French aeronauts?" In less than two hours we reached Louvain, having journeyed at the rate of about eighty-eight miles an hour. *

It all happened a century ago, and yet there is something in the very flamboyance and gaiety of the author's words which remind one of the French spirit in more recent wars. Whoever wants to know something more about ballooning in the nineteenth century should read de Fonvielle.

*Ibid.

133

Chapter 11

Higher and yet higher

To follow the development of scientific ballooning from the beginning of the nineteenth century we have to retrace our steps to the time when such popular showmen as Green were displaying their skill and prowess. As that distinguished Victorian scientist James Glaisher commented, the balloon had "degenerated into an instrument of popular exhibition and passing amusement, so that its striking characteristics and important bearing on science were in danger of fading completely from view."

What were these "striking characteristics"? First, a well-managed balloon in the hands of a capable aeronaut could rise high into the upper atmosphere and make scientific observations of the climatic conditions of that region. Second, it could explore air currents and take samples of air at different heights. Third, it could measure the earth's magnetic field and establish whether or not this varied with height. And all this could be done without climbing high mountains under arduous physical conditions, encumbered with packs and other gear.

Some facts were thought to be known already. Mountaineers carrying thermometers and barometers believed that the temperature of the atmosphere fell by one degree for every 300 feet of ascent, and that the atmospheric pressure decreased in a regular progression as one rose above sea level. The high-flying balloon could test these beliefs more rapidly and accurately than mountaineers; or so the scientists believed.

For instance, Camille Flammarion, a distinguished French savant (1842–1925), wrote: "This marvellous world of air, so mild and yet so strong, where tempests, whirlwinds, snow, and hail are elaborated, was henceforth opened to the inhabitants of terrestial soil. Its secrets would be disclosed, and the movements of the atmospheric world be counted, measured, and determined."

The first requisite of the scientific balloonist was to carry scientific measuring instruments aloft with him. These usually consisted of a Torricelli barometer (with a mercury column), a thermometer, a hygrometer, a magnetized needle for measuring the earth's magnetic field, a clock, and other instruments. There was seldom sufficient space in the balloon car for the scientist, his apparatus, and the aeronaut. In addition, the effect of oxygen shortage at high altitudes was not fully understood, and when the aeronauts rose, as they did, from three to five miles high, their judgment and powers of observation were often impaired by the scarcity of oxygen. Also the instruments tended to behave erratically at great heights.

These scientific aeronauts could judge the height they achieved only by the use of barometers, which were a kind of primitive altimeter. Etienne Robertson, in 1804, claimed to have reached a height of 23,526 feet, higher than anything attained before, but many believed him to be a charlatan. Then two young French scientists,

J. B. Biot and J. L. Gay-Lussac, made what many believe to have been the first truly scientific ascent. They rose from the Conservatoire des Arts et Métiers on August 24th, 1804, to a height of 25,000 feet, according to their barometer. It must be understood, however, that this system of registering the height by observing the barometric pressure was based on a theory of the French scientist Pascal, who had not allowed for variations in pressure due to meteorological conditions at varying heights.

Although it was not a strictly scientific ascent, no book on balloons could fail to mention the extraordinary feat of a young Frenchman named Arban. In 1846, in a frail car of basketwork, Arban crossed the Alps at night, borne aloft by a storm which thundered around him just before takeoff on the French side of that terrifying mountain barrier. Even today, when jet aircraft regularly fly over the Alps at an enormous height, the sight of those gigantic, snow-covered peaks and of the yawning crevasses between them can excite considerable unease.

Lacking a written firsthand account by the twenty-six-year-old aeronaut himself, we find the best description of his feat in de Fonvielle:

> The fantastic light of the moon spread a silver veil over the scene, and cast gigantic shadows from the lofty mountains. A cloud of floating snow threatened to precipitate the balloon into the enormous crevasses of the Mer de Glace. In the midst of this terrible situation a curious idea crossed the brain of this man, who ran the risk of being crushed among the glaciers. He threw

out a bottle in order that this fragile thing, falling among the snows, might serve as a witness to future centuries that a French aeronaut had crossed there. When daylight dawned, a splendid spectacle was revealed to the aerial voyager, who, struggling all night against the fearful cold, had thrown out bit by bit the ballast which was his salvation, and had thus cleared the peaks against which the ceaseless storm threatened to dash him. When viewed from below the various branches of the Alpine chain appear a mass of confusion, but seen from above their summits are seen to be arranged in regular and harmonious lines. Arban, half-stupefied, contemplated the harmony of these wonderful crests, which as one great whole lay spread out at his feet.*

Arban landed near the village of Pionforte, about four miles from Turin, and was warmly welcomed by the peasants; the same evening he received a great ovation when he appeared at a Turin theatre. He must have risen to a height exceeding 15,000 feet to clear the highest peaks, unless he was fortunate enough to float through the valleys which separate them.

Through the forties and fifties of the nineteenth century, the craze to establish altitude records grew. At one time, the desire had been to travel farthest; now it was to ascend highest. The higher regions of the upper atmosphere were uncharted territory, and, as in our own so-called Space Age, men vied with each other as to who should be first to explore it. The scientists were

* W. de Fonvielle, *Adventures in the Air* (London, 1877).

137

more interested in this struggle than were the showmen-aeronauts.

A number of such ascents were made on the Continent. The Astronomer Royal of Naples, Carlo Brioschi, after ascending from Padua with the aeronaut Andreoli, claimed to have registered a barometer reading of eight inches; if accurate, this reading represented an altitude of 30,000 feet, but this is doubtful. However, the two men probably rose to over 20,000 feet before their balloon burst (it was a combined gas-and-fire balloon similar to that in which Pilâtre de Rozier met his death). They parachuted to earth under the torn envelope; Andreoli survived, but Brioschi died from his injuries.

Two French amateur aeronauts, Barral and Bixio, achieved a remarkable altitude on July 25th, 1850, after ascending from Coulommiers, about thirty miles from Paris. Barral, the scientist, was lecturer in chemistry at the Paris Polytechnic School; his non-scientific colleague, Bixio, edited an agricultural magazine and presumably went along for the ride. They took registering barometers and thermometers with them and recorded some remarkable results. One was the extreme cold experienced, far greater than had been anticipated. At about 20,000 feet the temperature was 15° Fahrenheit, and they were surrounded by cloud; on their rising to 23,000 feet, the temperature dropped to −38°, or seventy degrees of frost. This was fifty degrees below the temperature which Gay-Lussac and Biot had recorded at the same altitude. "In the height of summer," wrote de Fonvielle, "it took them less than an hour to find, above Paris, the fine snow which indicates an ultra-polar temperature . . . they saw, dancing around their car, a cloud

Just before the *Zenith* tragedy, April 15th, 1875. Tissandier, Crocé-Spinelli and Sivel shown before the fatal descent

formed of fine needles of ice, which was in fact the kind of fleecy cloud known as cirrus. . . . These thousands of particles, so beautifully sculptured, radiate from a distance the cold of the impenetrable zone where they are formed." *

The two aeronauts had encountered what the modern pilot calls "icing cloud"—one of the reasons why modern aircraft are equipped with de-icers. They were not the first to observe this phenomenon, which can occur at lower altitudes. When Madame Blanchard came down after one of her ascents, her face was covered with ice crystals.

In 1851 the British Association for the Advancement of Science, Britain's leading scientific body, at last began to take an interest in aerostatics. One of their members, John Welsh of the Kew Meteorological Observatory, commissioned the veteran aeronaut Charles Green to take him on high-altitude flights in the *Nassau,* the very same balloon which had made the historic flight to Germany in 1836. Green, now in his seventies and living in a handsome house in Highgate called Aerial Villa, was highly complimented, as he had always wanted to use his balloon for the advancement of science. He had, in fact, made earlier high-altitude attempts on behalf of a wealthy country gentleman named George Rush, of Elsenham Hall, Essex, and had once reached a height of five miles. On that occasion, though they may not have known it, Rush, Green, and their companion, a young man named Spencer, had come perilously near the height at which men cannot survive without extra oxygen. When they returned safely to earth, at South-over, near Lewes, they complained of nausea, bleed-

* W. de Fonvielle, *Adventures in the Air* (London, 1877).

140

ing from the nose and ears, and acutely cold feet and hands. But they suffered no prolonged aftereffects.

Welsh and Green made four ascents with instruments, the highest recorded height being 22,930 feet. The death of Welsh, in 1859, brought this series of experiments to an end without very important results, and the British Association lost interest. It was then that the scientist James Glaisher, Fellow of the Royal Society, began to interest himself in balloons. He had studied aeronautics for a great number of years and was, in his time, probably the most thoroughly scientific aeronaut the world had produced. His aim was not adventure, let alone showmanship, but scientific observation from greater heights than had hitherto been attained. He wrote:

A taste for these studies was first developed during my residence in Ireland, in the years 1829 and 1830. At this time I was engaged on the principal triangulation of Trigonometrical Survey of Ireland and in the performance of my duty, I was often compelled to remain, sometimes for long periods, above, or enveloped in cloud. I was thus led to study the colours of the sky, the delicate tints of the clouds, the motion of opaque masses, the forms of crystals of snow. . . . I have watched with great interest the forms of the clouds, and often, when a barrier of cloud has suddenly concealed the stars from view, I have wished to know the cause of their rapid formation. *

Glaisher's most memorable ascent was made in the

* This and the following quotations from James Glaisher are taken from his book entitled *Travels in the Air* (London, 1871).

year 1862, when he was fifty-three years old. When he first planned to make scientific observations at great heights, he intended to employ two young men as scientific observers and a professional aeronaut as pilot. He first approached the veteran Charles Green, by now living in retirement, but the *Nassau* balloon, which Green kept in a shed in his garden, was found to be too worn and porous to be of service for high-altitude ascents.

Glaisher then sought the help of a younger aeronaut named Henry Coxwell, a professional of great experience. He and Glaisher got on well together despite their difference in age. After the disappointment concerning Green's veteran balloon, Coxwell volunteered to supervise the manufacture of a new and even larger aerostat, made of oilcloth, not silk, and very airworthy. Its capacity was 90,000 cubic feet, 20,000 more than that of the *Nassau*. Since the British Association had invested money in the enterprise, Glaisher, despite his advancing years, decided to make the ascent himself, accompanied by Coxwell as pilot. Glaisher prepared a number of scientific instruments and himself listed their purpose:

> (1) Determining the temperature of the dew-point by Daniell's dew-point hygrometer, by Regnault's condensing hygrometer, and by dry and wet bulb thermometers as ordinarily used, as well as when under the influence of the aspirator (so that considerable volumes of air could be made to pass over both their bulbs) at different elevations.

142

(The hygrometers were instruments for measuring the moisture content of the air; the aspirator—a pump worked by foot bellows—was to cool the thermometers, which would also be shielded from the direct rays of the sun.)

(2) To compare the readings of an aneroid barometer with that of a mercurial barometer up to five miles.

(3) To examine the electrical condition of the air up to five miles.

(4) To determine the oxygenic condition of the atmosphere by means of ozone papers.

(5) To determine whether the horizontal intensity of the earth's magnetism was less or greater with elevation by the time of the vibration of a magnet.

(6) To determine whether the solar spectrum when viewed from the earth, or far above it, exhibited any difference, and whether there were a greater or less number of dark lines crossing it, especially at sunset.

(7) To collect air at different elevations.

(8) To note the height of clouds and their density and thickness . . .

. . . and so on and so on, down to paragraph 13: "To note atmospherical phenomena in general, and to make general observations."

How cold and prosaic all these scientific observations sound compared with the thrill of taking off in a balloon from Vauxhall Gardens at night, with a giggling girl friend, well fortified with champagne, and hearing the crowd roar the popular music-hall song of the time:

Up in a balloon!
Up in a balloon!
Sailing round the little stars
Underneath the moon!

—to see London's myriad lights far below, then the dark countryside, and to end, perhaps, with a riotous evening in an Essex pub after a smooth landing. This is what ballooning, in the 1860s, meant to the mass of Londoners.

Glaisher and Coxwell made their ascent on September 5th, 1862, not from Vauxhall, Cremorne Gardens, the Crystal Palace, or any other of London's night haunts, but from the Wolverhampton gasworks, in the heart of England. Glaisher had chosen this site because the balloon would thus be less likely, after drifting in the higher atmosphere, to land in the sea.

The instruments prepared by Glaisher were fixed to the table lashed across the balloon's basket, and he attended to his precious instruments while Coxwell prepared to take off. How high they were about to ascend neither of them knew, but they hoped it would be as high as possible, higher than any human being had ever ascend before.

No description of mine could possibly equal that of Professor Glaisher himself, which I shall quote in some detail:

At 1 hour 13 minutes we entered a dense cloud of about 1,100 feet in thickness where the temperature fell to 36.5 degrees, the dew-point being the same, this indicating that the air here was saturated with moisture. At this point the report of a gun was heard. Momentarily the clouds became lighter, and on emerging from them at 1 hour 17 minutes, a flood of strong sunlight burst upon us with a beautiful blue sky without cloud, and beneath us lay a magnificent sea of clouds, its surface varied with endless hills, hillocks and mountain chains. I attempted to take a view with the camera but we were rising at too great a rapidity and revolving too quickly to enable me to succeed. The brightness of the clouds, however, was so great that I should have needed only a momentary exposure.

Higher still soared the balloon; and, as Coxwell threw out more ballast, the great envelope, now almost fully distended by expansion, strained at the network of ropes. Yet even at this height they could distinctly hear sounds coming from the ground. Somewhere, far, far below, lay Staffordshire with its factories, the fecund fields of Warwickshire and Worcestershire, the Malvern and the Cotswood hills. Below lay Victorian England in the mid-nineteenth century, but Glaisher and Coxwell, though they did not know it, were venturing into territory which was not to be fully explored until a hundred years later. Wrapped warmly in their Victorian clothing, with their quaint brass-bound instruments before them, they were being given a glimpse of what we, in the Jet Age, can see whenever we make a long-distance flight—but we fly in pressurized cabins, protected and indifferent.

The height of three miles was attained at 1 hour 28 minutes, with a temperature of 18 degrees Fahrenheit, and a dew-point of 13 degrees. At 1 hour 34 minutes Mr. Coxwell was panting for

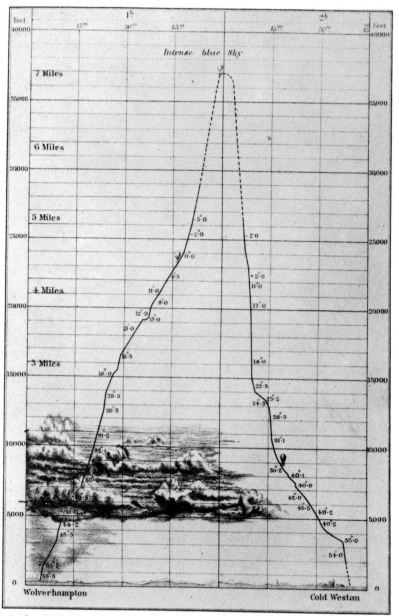

Path of Glaisher's balloon in its ascent from Wolverhampton to Cold
Weston near Ludlow, September 5th, 1862

breath; at 1 hour 38 minutes, the mercury of Daniell's hygrometer fell below the limits of the scale. We reached the elevation of four miles at 1 hour 40 minutes; the temperature was 8 degrees, the dew-point minus 15 degrees, or 47 degrees below the freezing point of water. Discharging ballast we in ten minutes attained the altitude of five miles, and the temperature had passed below zero and then read minus two degrees.

Of Glaisher's observation the scientist Hildebrandt observed that "he carried out the following observations in 1 hour 26 minutes: 107 readings of the mercury barometer, a similar number of the thermometer, 62 readings of the aneroid, 4 of the dry, and 86 of the wet-bulb thermometer, 62 of the gridiron barometer, 13 of the dry and 12 of the wet-bulb thermometer fitted with the aspirator [which he had to pump with the foot bellows] besides several observations with the hygrometer, and noting the time on 165 separate occasions."

Still the balloon continued to rise, while Coxwell watched the huge envelope swaying above them and occasionally threw out yet more ballast. Up to now neither aeronaut had experienced much difficulty in breathing, although Coxwell, who had the more physical work to do, had begun to pant. But now they were approaching a region which no human beings had known before, where the oxygen which sustains life on earth gets very thin. The theory of this rarefaction of the atmosphere was already known, of course, but, apart from mountaineers encumbered with their packs, few had experienced it.

Having discharged sand we ascended still higher; the aspirator became troublesome to work, and I also found a difficulty in seeing clearly. At 1 hour 51 minutes or later I read the dry-bulb thermometer as minus 5 degrees; after this I could not see the column of mercury nor the hands of the watch. I asked Mr. Coxwell to help me read the instruments. In consequence, however, of the rotary motion of the balloon . . . the valve line had become entangled, and he had to leave the car and mount into the ring to readjust it. I then looked at the barometer and found its reading to be 9.4 inches, still decreasing fast, implying a height exceeding 29,000 feet [somewhat higher than the average jet airliner flies in 1969].

Shortly after this I laid my arm upon the table, possessed of its full vigour, but on being desirous of using it I found it powerless—it must have lost its power momentarily. Trying to move the other arm I found it powerless also. Then I tried to shake myself and succeeded, but I seemed to have no limbs. In looking at the barometer my head fell over my left shoulder; I struggled and shook my body again, but could not move my arms. Getting my head upright for an instant only, it fell on my right shoulder; then I fell backwards, my back resting against the side of the car and my head on its edge.

Still the balloon continued to rise. There was no sound except the creaking of the ropes. As in a mist Glaisher saw Coxwell poised in the ring above the car, trying to open the valve to release gas. His arms were powerless to reach the rope. Glaisher must have recognized that death must be near, for he wrote afterwards:

> I dimly saw Mr. Coxwell, and endeavoured to speak but could not. In an instant intense darkness overcame me, so that the optic nerve lost power suddenly, but still I was conscious, with as active a brain as at the present moment when I am writing this. I thought I had been seized with asphyxia, and believed I should experience nothing more; other thoughts were entering my mind, when I suddenly became unconscious, as on going to sleep. I cannot tell anything of the sense of hearing, as no sound reached the ear to break the perfect stillness and silence of the regions between six and seven miles above the earth. My last observations were made at 1 hour 54 minutes, above 29,000 feet. I suppose two or three minutes to have elapsed between my eyes becoming insensible to seeing fine divisions at 1 hour 54 minutes, and then two or three minutes to have passed till I was insensible, which, I think, therefore, took place between about 1 hour 56 minutes and 57 minutes.

Coxwell, the younger man, the professional balloon pilot, had climbed into the rigging in an attempt to open the release valve, which was operated by a cord. Finding his arms paralyzed, his hands frozen, and hoarfrost gathered round the neck of the balloon, he inched forward and clenched the rope between his teeth. He dipped his head, once, twice, three times, and the last time he heard the valve open and the imprisoned gas roar into the sparse atmosphere.

Victorian altitude record: Henry Coxwell and James Glaisher in
trouble on their scientific ascent September 5th, 1862

A minute or so passed, and then Glaisher became aware of Coxwell speaking to him. He could only make out the words "temperature" and "observation."

> Returning consciousness came at 2 hours 7 minutes P.M. I found the water in the vessel supplying the wet-bulb thermometer one solid mass of ice. . . . Mr. Coxwell told me while in the ring he felt it piercingly cold, and that on attempting to leave the ring he found his hands frozen. He had, therefore, to place his arms on the ring and drop down by my side, and saw that my countenance was serene and placid . . . then it struck him that I was insensible. He wished to approach me but could not, and when he found insensibility coming upon him too, he became anxious to open the valve; ultimately he succeeded by seizing the cord with his teeth.
>
> No inconvenience followed my insensibility; and when we dropped it was in a country where no conveyance of any kind was to be had and I had to walk between seven and eight miles. During the descent, which was at first rapid, the wind was easterly. To check the rapidity of the descent, sand was thrown out at 2 hours 30 minutes. . . . The final descent took place in the centre of a large grass field belonging to Mr. Kersall, at Cold Weston, seven and a half miles from Ludlow.

Glaisher made many more ascents, from several of which he narrowly escaped with his life, but few examples of cold human courage could surpass the one just described.

Chapter 12

The attempt to reach the North Pole

The story which we now have to tell is perhaps the strangest in the history of aeronautics, especially as it was not revealed until thirty years after the events took place.

In July 1897, if you had chanced to visit a place called Dane's Island, within the Arctic Circle to the northwest of Spitsbergen, you would have seen an extraordinary sight. On the shore of this small, conical island, at the foot of snow-covered mountains, was a huge wooden shed, or hangar, open at one side. Through the open side an enormous balloon of elliptical shape was visible, and near it a number of men were working.

There was considerable activity in the narrow strait between the Norsk Islands. Several ships were anchored there, including the steamer *Virgo* with a crew of thirty men under the command of Captain H. Zachau. The *Virgo*, anchored within two hundred yards of the hangar, was the headquarters vessel of the Andrée Polar Expedition, whose leader, Salomon August Andrée, with two fellow Swedes, Nils Strindberg and Knut Fraenkel, was going to attempt to reach the North Pole by balloon. He even believed that, with favourable winds, he could continue past the North Pole, crossing the desolate wastes of the Arctic ice, and land eventually somewhere in Alaska near the Bering Strait.

At that time no one had ever reached the North Pole, or got anywhere near it. The days of Peary and Amundsen lay well ahead. There seemed at the time to be only two possible ways of reaching the Pole: one was by sledge, drawn by dogs or men; the other, which was being tried by Fridtjof Nansen, was to take a ship into the pack ice during summer, when the ice was broken up, allow oneself to be frozen in as winter came, and then drift with the slow-moving ice to the Pole and beyond.

To the men of the late nineteenth century the Pole was a perpetual challenge—especially to those, like the Swedes and Norwegians, whose lands lay near or within the Arctic Circle. The dangers and hazards were formidable. Little grows in those icy wastes. Fish can be caught through holes in the ice; but, apart from polar bears, seals, walruses, and sea birds, there is no other food. Explorers had to carry all provisions for their long journey and be prepared to spend an entire winter in temperatures far below zero in a land of perpetual ice and snow. Yet the Polar regions, like the highest mountains and the remotest jungles, drew men of spirit just because they had hitherto remained unconquerable.

Andrée, the leader of the expedition, was forty-three, a powerfully built man with strong, rather autocratic features. Trained as an engineer, he had developed an early interest in aeronautics, especially after he had visited America in 1876 and met that veteran aeronaut John Wise. Wise had always clung to his belief that a transatlantic crossing by balloon was feasible, and it is possible that Andrée conceived his plan of reaching

Salomon A. Andrée

the North Pole by balloon as a result of conversations with him.

Nils Strindberg, only twenty-five, was a physicist and had been Assistant in Physics at the University of Stockholm, but he had a second interest: photography. From the age of sixteen the art of photography had fascinated him, and in 1895 he had won first prize at an exhibition of photographs in Stockholm. Of the same family as the famous playwright August Strindberg, he was something of an artist as well as a scientist. He loved music and was a competent performer. Also, unlike his two companions, neither of whom was married or engaged, Strindberg had a fiancée and hoped to be married on his return from the expedition.

The third member of the expedition, Knut Fraenkel, was twenty-seven, a young athlete with a powerful frame and a love of mountain-climbing and other outdoor activities. More extrovert than his two companions, Frankel

154

had intended to become an army officer, and in 1896, the year before the expedition, he had passed his examination as a civil engineer. He had become interested in the reports of a series of earlier experiments Andrée had conducted in a somewhat smaller balloon, the *Svea*, in which he had crossed the Baltic Sea. When in 1896 a certain Dr. Ekholm, who was to have flown with Andrée to the Pole, had to withdraw, Fraenkel sought an interview and offered to take Ekholm's place. Andrée liked the young man and engaged him.

On Andrée's instructions both Strindberg and Fraenkel had gone to Paris (where, incidentally, the Polar balloon was made under the supervision of a Swedish engineer), had studied aeronautics under competent instructors, and had made several ascents.

Years of hard work, effort, and thought had preceded that July day when the *Eagle* (in Swedish, *Ornen*) strained at her cables in the hangar on Dane's Island, and the aeronauts, having waited weeks for a suitable wind, decided that the long-hoped-for moment had come.

Andrée had begun by arousing the interest of well-known explorers and men of science. One of these was Baron N. A. E. Nordenskjöld, a renowned explorer and the discoverer of the Northeast Passage, who showed great interest in the aeronaut's proposals and approved of them. Another supporter was the great Alfred Nobel. Andrée had to use all his powers of persuasion to convince people that his scheme was sound; and, as the Swedes are a hard-headed race, he had to give them hard scientific facts and be ready to answer every objection. On February 13th, 1895, in a lecture given to the Academy of Sciences at Stockholm, he pointed out the difficulties which earlier explorers had had in penetrating the ice-filled Polar Sea. Nansen was making an attempt in a strongly built ship, the *Fram*, which he hoped would be carried by the slow-moving currents of ice. Other attempts had been made with sledges but had not been successful up to that date.

Andrée then boldly outlined his plan, which was to be carried in a balloon to the North Pole, and not, he added, "the steerable balloon which has been hoped for but not yet achieved, but the balloon as we now have it, modified in certain ways so that it can be *partially* steered." He then stated the four main conditions which, in his opinion, were essential for the success of the expedition. These, briefly summarized, were : (a) The balloon must be able to carry three persons, all the necessary scientific equipment and cameras for taking observations, three sledges, a collapsible boat, tents, guns, ammunition, and provisions for not less than three months; this last would be needed if an accident forced the aeronauts to walk over the pack ice to the nearest land. (b) The balloon must be absolutely gas-tight so that it could remain aloft for thirty days. (c) The balloon must be filled with hydrogen at some place in the Arctic tracts. (d) The balloon must be partially steerable.

The distance from Spitsbergen to the Bering Strait is about 650 miles, and Andrée believed that the journey could be accomplished in six days.

Of course, there were objections to these beliefs. How on earth could a balloon be steered when it was subject to the whims of the wind? Andrée's answer was to use a more sophisticated form of the guide rope which the aeronaut Charles Green had used fifty years earlier: instead of one rope there would be several, attached to a swivel below the car. On each side of the lower part of the balloon would be a sail. The angle of the sails could be set, in relation to the wind, by adjusting the guide ropes in such a way as to rotate the balloon itself.

The idea was *not* to let the balloon fly freely in the upper atmosphere, but to keep it at a steady height. Its weight would have to be so adjusted, by use of the ropes, that it would remain at a height of about 800 feet above the earth's surface. If it tended to rise too high, the weight of the guide ropes would bring it down again. If it swooped too low, it would be relieved of the weight of the part of the ropes trailing across the ice and would tend to rise. Ballast could also be thrown out to assist ascent, and in addition to the guide ropes there would also be shorter draglines to serve a similar purpose when the balloon was at a low altitude.

How would this affect the steering? Aeronauts had tried fitting sails to balloons before, but they never worked because a free balloon travels as fast as the wind which blows it along; it is itself a huge sail, and any additional sails are pointless. The reason why a sailing boat can be steered is that *it is travelling much more slowly than the wind;* the friction of the water through which it passes slows it down so that it can never attain the wind's velocity. Direction can therefore be altered by altering the trim of the sails and by the use of the rudder, which is itself a friction device. One function of Andrée's guide rope dragging across the ice and sea would be to slow down the balloon to well below wind speed. Andrée's theory was that, under these conditions, the sails, projecting on each side of the lower hemisphere of the balloon, just above the car, could be used to alter direction. He admitted that complete control would not be possible; there was no question of being able to make a right-angled turn, let alone to turn round and go back, but from previous experiments in the *Svea* he calculated that a change of course of up to twenty-seven degrees would be possible. So he would not be entirely at the mercy of the wind.

Then the critics raised objections. What would happen if snow and ice formed on the envelope and weighed it down? Andrée replied that he proposed to make his attempt in summer and that the total rainfall during June, July, and August amounts to less than six pounds per square foot. He also pointed out that the temperature, in summer, hovers around the freezing point ($32°$ Fahrenheit); that above this temperature snow is soon melted by the sun; and that below it any snow which fell would quickly blow away because the balloon would be moving more slowly than the wind.

As an additional precaution he proposed to cover the whole upper hemisphere of the balloon with a *calotte*, or hood, of silk, which would prevent snow and ice from collecting in the flat spaces between the ropes imprisoning the envelope; also, the effect of the guide ropes and draglines would be to shake the balloon at times, thus dispersing the snow. He had apparently thought of everything, and his audiences were impressed.

Andrée wound up his lecture by saying: "It is not only possible to carry out a balloon journey across the Polar tracts, but there is very much in favour of making an effort to do so. By a single balloon journey, we shall be able to gain a greater knowledge of the Arctic regions than can be obtained in centuries by any other way. . . ."

And now, on a fine summer day, July 11th, 1897, all was ready for the ascent. The balloon had been tested and found to be gas-tight. Within the car, which was cylindrical, were three berths for the aeronauts, and on top of the car, which was railed off, was an observation platform like the bridge of a ship. In containers slung from the ropes were all the instruments that the aeronauts required: chronometers, chronographs, barometers, hygrometers, compasses, thermometers, a sextant, a theodolite, a pair of field glasses, and Strindberg's photographic apparatus, including an opaque sack (in lieu of a darkroom) for loading and unloading the photographic plates.

There were also ballast, grapnels, anchors, buoys to carry messages, thirty-six carrier pigeons for the same purpose, a Primus stove for cooking (to be slung well below the balloon in flight and lit by remote control), provisions for three and a half months, tents and tent poles, three sledges, a collapsible boat, and a medicine chest.

The wind was favourable, blowing strongly from the south. Andrée, Fraenkel, Strindberg, and their collaborators went ashore from the *Virgo* and examined the *Eagle* from the roof of the hangar. Andrée asked, "Shall we try or not?" Strindberg, who had already written a letter of farewell to his fiancée, replied, "I think we should attempt it." Fraenkel, at first doubtful, finally agreed with the other two.

The weather was almost perfect. On the *Virgo* a

toast was drunk in champagne to the success of the Andrée Polar Expedition. Everyone was jubilant, especially the sailors of the *Virgo*. The *Eagle*, freed from its hangar, rose to a good height, restrained by its mooring ropes. Ballast had been taken on board and every item of equipment carefully checked. The moment had come.

Andrée shouted "Cut away the ropes everywhere." Three knives cut the ropes holding down the carrying ring, and the *Eagle* rose into the clear sky. The men on the *Virgo* watched it rise, then swoop, almost dipping into the sea as the strong wind carried it northward. The aeronauts threw out ballast, and the *Eagle* soared again, bearing away swiftly to the north until it was lost to view. The sailors on the *Virgo* stopped cheering.

It was within three years of the beginning of the twentieth century. In Germany, powered airship flights had already been made with the newly invented internal-combustion engine developed by Gottlieb Daimler. In the United States, Wilbur and Orville Wright were already making experiments which would result in the world's first heavier-than-air aircraft. But up in the Far North, Andrée, Fraenkel, and Strindberg were venturing their lives in a free balloon, little different except in size and detail from those which had flown from Versailles and the Champ-de-Mars 114 years earlier.

And then a sailor from the *Virgo* came running up from the shore with the cry, "The draglines are still lying here on the shore!" By that time the *Eagle* was well out of sight, heading towards the Pole.

The Andrée Expedition; the balloon sets off from Danes Island, July 11th, 1897

Chapter 13

The flight of
the *Eagle*

The short draglines which were intended to help steer the balloon had been laid out along the shore below the hangar to the east (with the idea of giving the balloon a start in that direction and so enabling it to clear the highest part of Amsterdam Island). At first it was thought that they must have broken when the *Eagle* took off, but this proved incorrect. At the suggestion of certain friends, who feared that the lines might catch in the ice and hold down the balloon, Andrée had incorporated in each line a section which could be unscrewed. In case the lines became caught fast, the upper third of each could be saved. Unhappily for Andrée and his companions, a fault in the lines, when the balloon rose, caused the three lines to unscrew themselves, leaving the lower two thirds of each line lying on the shore and so reducing the possibility of steering. However, the longer guide ropes were not damaged, and the observers on the *Virgo* watched them cutting a wake through the sea, like that of a ship, as the *Eagle* disappeared into the distance.

After the balloon had lifted into the sky above Spitsbergen and been lost to view, the press and the people of Sweden, and indeed of Europe, waited expectantly for news. Radio telegraphy had not been invented, but Andrée had devised two methods of passing on reports of his progress. A small metal cylinder containing a message could be placed in the tail feathers of the carrier pigeons he had with him, and it was agreed that Strindberg should send regular dispatches to the Stockholm newspaper *Aftonbladet*. The second method was to put messages inside buoys made of cork surrounded by a copper netting and then to drop the buoys, in the hope that they would be found by someone who would pass them on.

At about one o'clock in the morning of July 15th, four days after the *Eagle* had left Dane's Island, the skipper of the Norwegian sealer *Alken* was called from his cabin because a "peculiar bird" had perched on the peak of the ship, having come in from the southward. Skipper Ole Hansen thought it was a ptarmigan and shot it; it fell overboard, and the ship sailed on. Later that day the *Alken* met another sealer, and Hansen mentioned this incident. Immediately the crew of the other ship asked whether perhaps it might have been a pigeon from Andrée's expedition.

Hansen was so struck by this possibility that he went back to the place at which the bird had been shot, lowered boats, and looked for it. By an extraordinary chance the body of the bird was found floating in the sea, and when it was examined the metal cylinder was found. Inside was this message, which later was published in the Swedish press:

From Andrée's Polar Expedition to the *Aftonbladet*, Stockholm. 13th July, 12:30 midday. Latitude 82 degrees 2 minutes. Longitude 15 degrees

5 minutes east. Good speed to east 10 degrees south. All well on board. This is the third pigeon post. Andrée.

That was the only message received by pigeon post from the *Eagle*. None of the other thirty-five pigeons was ever recovered. The little bird, now stuffed and mounted, stands today in a museum alongside the cylinder which carried this one message. There was, however, no shorthand dispatch from Strindberg, as had been expected.

Week after week the world waited for news of Andrée and his companions, but there was complete silence. When the thirty days had passed by (the time the balloon could have remained aloft), it was presumed that the aeronauts had been forced down somewhere on the Arctic ice. They had taken sledges, tents, and provisions against such an emergency, and there was always a chance that, if they managed to endure the winter, they would turn up somewhere. Hope was not entirely lost, and searching parties were sent out. But, when the year 1898 passed without any further news, it was realized that they must have perished, no one knew where.

There was a poignant moment in 1899, when on May 14th, 672 days after being thrown from the *Eagle*, one of Andrée's message-buoys was found in the Kollfjord on the north coast of Iceland. The message was dated July, 11th 1897—the date of departure—and simply read:

This buoy has been thrown from Andrée's balloon at 10:35 GMT [Greenwich mean time] on July 11th, 1897, in about 82 degrees latitude and 25 degrees longitude east from Greenwich. We are at a height of about 2,000 feet. All well, Andrée, Strindberg, Fraenkel.

Over a year later a second buoy was picked up in Finnmark, Norway, by a woman searching for wreckage on the coast. The buoy had floated for three years in the sea. The message inside, in Andrée's handwriting, was intact and had evidently been written on the day of departure. It read:

Our journey has hitherto gone well. We are still moving on at a height of 830 feet, in a direction which first was N. 10 degrees declination, but later N. 45 degrees declination. Four carrier pigeons were sent off at 5:40 G.M.T. They flew westerly. We are now over the ice, which is much broken up. Weather magnificent. In best of humours. Andrée, Strindberg, Fraenkel.

At the bottom of the message a sentence in Strindberg's writing read: "Above the clouds since 7:45 GMT."

By this time the message was only of historical interest. Three years had passed since the *Eagle* had risen from Dane's Island, and no one knew, or was likely to know, how far the balloon had flown or what had been the fate of the three aeronauts. Andrée had passed into history, and his name represented only another Polar expedition which had failed, on this occasion with fatal results.

Continued efforts were made to reach the North and the South Poles, by ship or on foot across the Polar ice. An American explorer, Robert E. Peary, made a successful journey to the North Pole from Greenland in 1909.

The Andrée Expedition; inspecting the balloon July 2nd, 1897

The South Pole was conquered by a Norwegian, Roald Amundsen, in 1911, and shortly thereafter (January 1912) by an Englishman, Robert F. Scott.

Two and a half years later the First World War broke out, a conflict which was to demolish completely what remained of the Victorian world to which Andrée belonged. When it ended, not only had great powered airships been used to bomb cities, but heavier-than-air craft had developed from Wilbur and Orville Wright's primitive machines into deadly weapons of war and also into a means of transport which was to overleap the barriers—mountains, seas, and deserts—which had hindered or prevented human communication ever since man appeared on earth. By comparison with aeroplanes, even the mighty airship seemed outdated, though it continued to be used on several fronts during the First World War.

In 1926 an American, Richard Evelyn Byrd, flew from Spitsbergen to the North Pole and back in sixteen hours, and two days later Roald Amundsen, with an Italian, Umberto Nobile, flew from Spitsbergen in the airship *Norge*, crossed the North Pole, and landed at Teller, Alaska, a distance of 3,391 miles, in seventy-one hours. In 1929, Richard Byrd and three companions flew from their base at Little America to the South Pole and returned successfully. All these achievements made Polar exploration seem somewhat less dangerous. They were part of the confident twentieth-century pattern in which machinery seemed to be mastering natural forces and conditions. In fact, they belong essentially to our own technological age.

The gulf between 1930 and 1897 was far greater than that between 1897 and 1797, and Andrée's Polar Expedition seemed as distant as the car is from the stagecoach. Yet in the summer of 1930 an eerie discovery opened a door on the almost forgotten past. A little ship called the *Bratvaag* was seal-hunting far out in the Arctic seas, near the coast of White Island, sometimes called New Iceland. Owing to pack ice, this island is usually inaccessible to ships, but that summer the hunters were able to anchor and go ashore. Some sailors, including the ship's skipper, had walked a hundred yards or so when they saw strange black objects protruding from the snow. There was a rectangular enclosure roughly built of stones and driftwood, in which a tent had stood; parts of the fabric were still there, and some of the floor covering. Within the enclosure, partly covered with ice, was a human skeleton, partially clothed. The upper part of the body had been eaten by Polar bears, and the head was missing. When the discoverers opened the remains of the tattered jacket, they found a large monogram A, and in one of the inside pockets was a diary in Andrée's handwriting, a lead pencil, and a pedometer (an instrument for measuring the distance covered by a walker).

Thirty yards away, also sticking out of the ice and partially filled with it, lay a canvas boat containing many objects. One of those which could be removed was a book. The skipper took it with him when he rejoined the ship. All he said was, "We have found Andrée." The book was Nils Strindberg's observation book, with detailed calculations of astronomical observations and other notes. Opening one page, the finders saw the words "The sledge journey, 1897." Overcome by the discovery, the crew stopped hunting seals and walruses, took mattocks and spades, and made their way back to the site, led by the skipper. Among them was the geologist Gunnar Horn, who wrote of this moment:

> We waded across the little stream and went silently toward the camp. Behind us the sea is calm and ice-free as far as the eye can reach. Glimmering white icebergs lie aground in the neighbourhood of the island. We approach the camp one by one, without exchanging many words. The excitement is great, for in a moment we shall stand in Andrée's last camp.
>
> We are here on the spot! Hither had Andrée and his comrades come, never to leave the place again. The moment was a strange, solemn one, and some moments passed before we began our task. . . . Our thoughts went back to that July day in 1897 when the *Eagle* rose from Dane's Island

in Spitsbergen with three men in the car, and
was carried away by the wind on the most daring
Polar expedition ever undertaken.*

Near Andrée's body lay a gun, buried in the ice,
and a Primus stove still partially filled with paraffin.
Horn wrote:

> When we pumped, the paraffin came out of
> the burner in a fine spray, and the valve at
> the side was in order too. We unscrewed it
> a little and could see how the gas streamed out.
> If it had been necessary to cook anything now
> we might perhaps have been able to use Andrée's
> thirty-three-year-old Primus. Besides this we saw
> a cup, cooking utensils, and an axe, and, in a little
> wooden box, a pot of lanoline.

This was the stove which, slung beneath the balloon
car, had cooked the meals of the aeronauts, as it had
also on their long, wearisome journey by sledge across
the pack ice to their last camp.

A few score yards away the party found another
body, which had been laid in an improvised grave. Horn
described it:

> First we saw a cranium which lay there,
> dreadfully smiling, among the stones, four yards
> from the grave. It was a typical Arctic grave. The
> corpse had been placed directly on the ground,
> in a crevice in the rocks, and then covered with
> stones. The feet in their Lapp boots stuck out

* *The Andrée Diaries* (John Lane The Bodley Head, London, 1931),
contribution by Gunnar Horn. The following quotations from Horn
and from members of the expedition are taken from this book.

between the stones, and, higher up, the left shoulder-blade was visible. Above the stones was found another shoulder-blade. It was evident that the bears had been busy there too.

From fragments of clothing bearing the monogram S, the discoverers assumed that this was the body of Nils Strindberg. A handkerchief bearing his initials was also found, not far away. Evidently he had died first and been buried by his comrades. But the crew of the *Bratvaag* found no trace of Fraenkel's body.

Returning to the boat, Horn noted, among other things, two shotguns, an anemometer, a parcel of scientific books, including nautical and trigonometrical tables, some string, a workbox with sewing materials, articles of clothing, a boat hook, and the bones of a Polar bear. Near the boat were some ammunition boxes full of cartridges, a rolled-up Swedish flag, a barometer, and an instrument box. And other objects could be seen dimly through the ice which more than half filled the boat. When they prized the vessel free of the ice, they found that it had been lashed to a sledge which lay beneath, and another empty sledge lay nearby.

With great difficulty, all these objects, and the human remains, were released from the ice and reverently carried to the *Bratvaag*, which steamed off for Tromsö, a port in northwestern Norway. There it was met by another ship, the *Michael Sars*, on board which was the commission appointed by the Swedish and Norwegian governments to receive and preserve the finds.

Not long afterwards another vessel, the *Isbjorn*, financed by the press, made its way to White Island in the hope of finding objects which the crew of the *Bratvaag*

The Andrée Expedition; after the forced landing, transporting the boat

had overlooked. This expedition found a third skeleton, which the journalist Stubbendorf described as "the upper part of the body and head of a man who was lying on his left side, and whose left arm was seen to be bent upwards, with the hand beneath the head. The dead man was frozen fast into the ground, and I gained the impression that he had lain embedded in the ice, deep below the surface, ever since death touched him." This could hardly be anything else than the body of Knut Fraenkel. It had lain within the rough enclosure a few yards from that of Salomon Andrée, but the sleeping bag which lay between them had not been used. Other remains of this body were scattered around, including the backbone, two thigh bones, and a foot. The two men had died where they lay, probably of cold and exhaustion, since there were ample provisions in the boat and the sledge and no lack of ammunition. A third sledge was found, together with Fraenkel's almanac and three memorandum books, Strindberg's logbook, some geological samples collected by Andrée, a bundle of clothing wrapped in balloon fabric, a sextant, a medicine chest, and numerous photographs taken by Strindberg. These too were taken back to Tromsö and handed over to the Swedish-Norwegian commission.

Besides the brief diary found in Andrée's pocket there was a much fuller one which described the course of the expedition from the moment it left Dane's Island to the first sighting of White Island, nearly four months later. The two diaries had suffered considerably from thirty-three years' exposure, particularly that found within Andrée's jacket, in which he had devoted a couple of pages to describing what had happened shortly after their arrival at their last camp. This, unhappily, was not clearly decipherable, but the other, larger diary was. So were parts of Strindberg's almanac, with its astronomical observations, and some letters written to his fiancée in Sweden. From these it is possible for us to reconstruct what is almost certainly the most courageous enterprise ever undertaken in a free, man-carrying balloon.

After the initial swoop almost into the sea, in which the car touched the water, the *Eagle* had risen rapidly to over 2,000 feet. Andrée was too occupied to keep notes for the first few hours, but Strindberg noted, in his almanac, "guide rope lost." They passed over Hollander Naze at 1:56 p.m. and after another twenty minutes found themselves over Vogelsan Island, where Strindberg threw down a tin containing a message for his fiancée. It has never been found.

During this "free-flight period" the aeronauts decided to try to make good the loss of part of the draglines by repairing them. They pulled up one of the ballast lines and began to splice it onto one of the draglines. While this work was going on, Nils Strindberg was busy taking photographs. Soon clouds enveloped the *Eagle*, which was still bearing steadily northeastward. Through gaps in the clouds the travellers could see drifting ice to the north and southwest. To the south, the great bulk of Spitsbergen disappeared gradually into the mist. And then the balloon began to sink, owing to the weight of ice on the envelope.

This did not greatly worry the voyagers, for they had intended to fly at a low altitude, trailing their guide ropes across the ice and thus reducing speed so that the sails could be used for directing the flight. At 5:36 p.m. they released the first four carrier pigeons. Ice floes were now seen, somewhat larger than before. The travellers came into sunshine again and then ate their first meal on board: sandwiches and broth, with macaroni. A soft whistling came from the large balloon valve, due to escaping gas caused by expansion in the sunshine. A few birds were seen, but otherwise nothing except clouds and ice. The only sounds were the shriek of seabirds, the low whistling of the valve, and occasionally, from far below, loud reports like gunfire—the sound of ice breaking up.

From Andrée's diary:

> Fog lightens a little and
> the balloon is rising.

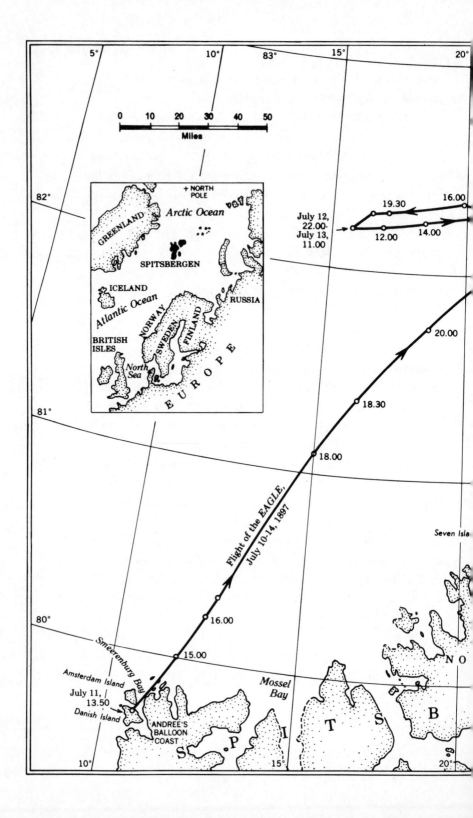

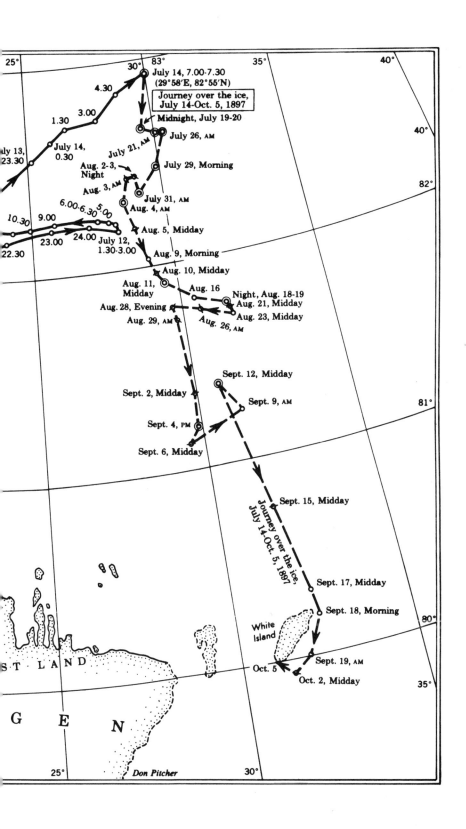

> Much that we have taken for
> open water was probably
> only snow-free and
> water-covered ice.
> 4 hours 55 o'clock
> movement continues incessantly
> course North 25 degrees [East] Magnetic
> at 5 o'clock I thought I heard a little auk
> And I saw a fulmar circle
> round us. He was not afraid. On
> . . . middle of back edge . . .
> . . . two white patches
> and on the beak or front part
> of the head was black
> course . . . 5 hours 5 o'clock (5567)

Later Strindberg and Fraenkel went to their berths for a few hours of sleep, while Andrée continued his watch from the railed-off roof of the car as the *Eagle* journeyed on through the Polar night:

> No land in sight. The horizon is
> not clear however. It is indeed a wonderful
> journey through the night. I am cold but
> will not wake the two sleepers. They
> need rest. We have still [not seen any]
> bear or seal. When
> the balloon descended the ropes
> did not lie straight and this
> makes the car
> swing backwards and makes the sails
> press down the Balloon. This is
> a pity for . . . does not

considerably.
Speed 0.8 (31.2 ins per second)
. . . Course North 50 degrees West Magnetic . . .

On the following morning, July 12th, at 6:00 a.m.
Andrée observed:

> . . . great seal (walrus?) two of them
> were seen. One of them grew frightened,
> the other not. The ice is traversed
> by leads of open water
> psychrom + 0.2 + 0.2
> Course North 80 degrees West Magnetic . . .

The leads—often mentioned—were great sea channels in the ice, which from the air looked like rivers. On that day, the second of their journey, the *Eagle*, having flown through freezing fog, descended even lower, and the guide ropes took the ice. The height varied from 330 feet to 65 feet. More ballast was thrown overboard, and, like an evil omen, a great black bird was seen circling the car. Now the fog became thicker, and it was impossible to see more than a mile ahead; nothing but ice, water, and still more ice, the most desolate landscape in the world. But the gas had stopped whining from the valve, and the aeronauts hoped that not too much had been lost.

> 7 hours 5 minutes the balloon stopped
> 7.10 it still remains motionless
> Psychr + 0.6 + 0.5. 7 hr o'clock
> 7 hrs. 15 o'clock a fulmar visible
> quite near the car
> The balloon not free

before 7 hrs 32 o'clock
and then went direct to West Magnetic.
Coffee made in 18 minutes . . .

All this time Strindberg had been taking photographs and making scientific observations in his logbook, while Fraenkel also, besides being the expedition's cook, kept his observations and took turns on watch so that the others could rest. At 11:13 on that morning more carrier pigeons were sent off, but they never reached their destination. There was light fog and a fine drizzle of rain. At about this time Andrée noted "blood-red ice below, probably the relics of a bear's meal." The *Eagle* continued to fly very low over the ice, and repeated attempts were made to get it to rise. More ballast was thrown overboard, then some knives, an iron anchor, and a ballast line, but to no avail.

The balloon was so heavily weighted with freezing fog that the car began to bump on the ice as it was dragged onwards by the slight wind.

12th July p.m.
mag. South 75 degrees West Magnetic 7/6 58
incessant fog and
bumpings every 5th minute
humour good
magn. South 80 degrees West 7 hrs. 3 o'clock
. . . Ice coarser and more
pressed than before
fog
Bad surface (ice)

At ten o'clock that evening the *Eagle* came to a halt, one of its guide ropes having caught in the ice. The balloon, the car, and the aeronauts were dripping with moisture. During the lull Andrée permitted himself to reflect on his situation in the diary:

> Although we could have thrown out ballast and although the wind might perhaps carry us to Greenland, we determined to be content with standing still. We have been obliged to throw out so much ballast today, have not had any sleep nor been allowed any rest from the repeated bumpings, and we probably could not have stood it much longer. All three of us must have a rest, and I have sent Strindberg and Fraenkel to bed at 11:20 o'clock and mean to let them sleep until 6 or 7 o'clock if I can manage to keep watch until then. . . . Is it not a little strange to be floating here above the Polar Sea? To be the first that have floated here in a balloon? How soon, I wonder, shall we have successors? Shall we be thought mad or will our example be followed? I cannot deny but that all three of us are dominated by a feeling of pride. We think we can well face death, having done what we have done. Is not the whole, perhaps, the expression of an extremely strong sense of individuality which cannot bear the thought of living and dying like a man in the ranks, forgotten by coming generations? Is this ambition?
>
> The rattling of the guide-lines in the snow and the flapping of the sails are the only sounds heard, except the whining [of wind] in the basket.

These were the only words in the whole of the diary

in which the explorer expressed his innermost thoughts; but they are enough. The Greek hero Odysseus would have understood what Andrée meant; his ideal was a life fulfilled in honourable and heroic action.

During the whole of that night of July 12th, the *Eagle* remained motionless, poised above the ice. Then the wind strengthened, and the balloon swayed, twisted, and turned, longing to be free. At last, at 10:55 a.m., the guide rope broke loose from the ice, and the *Eagle* lumbered on, still very low, with repeated bumpings of the car upon the ice.

Strindberg climbed into the carrying ring above the car and wrote a letter to his fiancée. It began:

> Up in the carrying ring it is confoundedly pleasant. One feels so safe there and so at home. One knows that the bumps up there are felt less, and this allows one to sit calmly and write without having to hold on.

Here follow eight lines which the editor of the *Andrée Diaries* has left as dots, presumably because he considered them too personal to be published; then there is a description of the preparations for the takeoff and the beginning of the flight. Strindberg did not write any more letters from the balloon although, in his almanac, he recorded:

> I tried to lie down in the car at 7 o'clock but in consequence of the bumping I became seasick. . . . Afterwards I went up to the carrying ring with Fraenkel. Threw out provisions as ballast. Fraenkel afterwards went to lie down at 9:00 o'clock. I took altitude of sun together with Andrée, who

was down in car, I in carrying ring. Then I opened my clothes-sack and put on an additional pair of balloon-cloth trousers and an Iceland jersey, intending to sleep. But first I read Anna's last letter. It was an enjoyable moment.

Before midday the balloon was aloft again, driving steadily onwards before an east-northeasterly wind. The spirits of the three comrades rose as Fraenkel prepared to cook a midday meal. The menu has been preserved in the diary and reads as follows:

> Dinner du 13 Juillet.
> Potage Hotch Potch.
> Chateaubriand
> The King's Special Ale
> Chocolate with Biscuits.
> Biscuits, raspberry syrup and H_2O.

Strindberg commented: "a good and invigorating meal!"

More carrier pigeons were sent off, and it was one of these which landed on the ship *Alken*. By about two in the afternoon they again ran into mist and freezing fog; the balloon descended, and soon the car began to bump against the ice. In order to lighten it, the aeronauts threw out another buoy and a box of medicine. For a time they hovered clear above the ice, and then at about six that evening the bumping began again; at eight that evening they threw out more objects, including six buoys, various provisions, 165 pounds of sand, and a winch. This time the balloon rose to a reasonable height, so that the sails could be refixed, and good progress was made. "Altogether it is quite splendid," Andrée commented in his diary.

But shortly after midnight the expedition's leader recorded:

> Our long guide-line has now broken off.
> Constant fog. No land and no birds, seals,
> or walruses.

And an hour later the balloon was bumping again.

> Monotonous, touch, new touch
> Another touch
> Bear-tracks, 2 hrs 6 minutes a.m.

So it continued throughout the day, until, at five minutes past six in the evening, evidently after more ballast had been thrown out, the balloon rose suddenly to a considerable height. The diary reads:

> Course North 55 degrees East 6 hrs. 5m. o'clock.
> 6.20 o'clock the balloon rose to a great height
> but we opened both valves and were down again
>   at 6.29 o'clock
> 8 hrs 11 o'clock we jumped out of the balloon.
> The landing
> 7 hours hard work had
> to be done before we could recreate ourselves.
> The Polar ice wears out the ropes more than our
> experience shows.

And in Strindberg's memorandum-almanac there occur just these few words:

> *July*
> 11. Sun.)
> 12. Mon.)Journeyed in the balloon.
> 13. Tu.   )

14. W.   Landed.
16. F.   ) Worked on the sledges and
          the boat.
17. S.   ) Nice days.

The balloon journey was over after a little less than three days. Owing to the weight of snow and ice and the loss of gas when the balloon was flying high, the *Eagle* could go no farther. The aeronauts had travelled to a point only about 250 miles from their starting place; but, owing to the varying winds, first northeastward, then westward, then eastward again, the mileage they had covered was considerably greater. They were almost at latitude 82 degrees, well north of the Arctic Circle, were far from any land, and were surrounded by drifting ice riven by leads.

They had sledges, provisions, guns, ammunition, and a canvas boat with which to traverse the leads when they could not drag their sledges over the pack ice. They were experienced navigators and had all the necessary instruments for plotting the journey back to Spitsbergen. Also it was still summer, during which the temperature rarely dropped much below the freezing point. It was going to be a tough journey, since they were faced, not with smooth, hard-frozen ice, but with broken-up floes interspersed by leads and with hill-like hummocks or ridges of "pressure ice."

Nonetheless, 250 miles is not a very great distance, even on foot, provided one can travel directly towards one's objective. But they knew, as all Polar explorers know, that this would not be possible, since the ice floes across which they were to travel were constantly shifting and the water they had to cross had strong currents. Nor would the ice always be strong enough to bear their weight. And there was always the knowledge that, if they did not reach Spitsbergen before October, at the latest, they would have to endure the long Arctic winter, if they could, holed up in a snow hut against the killing cold.

So, after a day spent in loading their provisions and equipment onto sledges, they set out southwestward across the drifting ice. Andrée's diary records that terrible journey, during which for two and a half months they never saw land. Every day they hauled their heavy sledges for hours across that desolate region of ice, sea, and snow hills, sometimes shooting birds or polar bears for food, halting to prepare a meal, and then moving on. Sometimes they crawled on all fours to test the sup-

The landing of the *Eagle*, July 14th, 1897

porting power of the ice; sometimes they transferred their sledges to the boat in order to cross a lead. At night they pitched their tent and crawled into it for warmth, shelter, and fitful sleep. From time to time one or another of the party fell ill and had to be dosed from the medicine chest. Sometimes one of them developed painful blisters on his feet, so that the other two would have to haul his sledge too. At times the sledges capsized in the water, and their contents had to be dried out. And every day the three men recorded the time, and took astronomical and meteorological observations.

Andrée rationed their food from the canned provisions they carried, and these, supplemented at times by the carcass of a bear, a seal, or a walrus, had to suffice. Life became contracted to the pursuit of food, as it was with primitive man. "Paradise," wrote Andrée, "is large level ice-floes with fresh-water pools full of water, with here and there a young polar bear with tender meat." On another occasion, August 7th, he wrote that he believed they had covered a greater distance than on any other day, about three miles, "though," he admitted, "the wind is right against us and has probably driven us just as far back." Despite these hardships, Strindberg continued to take his photographs, and Andrée fished up biological and geological specimens from the pools and put them carefully into labelled containers. He remained the man of science throughout the journey.

Now Strindberg is sitting mending trousers in the seat, and Fraenkel is oiling guns. Fraenkel's stomach pains are now over.

Andrée explained the art of pulling a sledge over the mixture of ice and water:

Wild crossings must often be made. The sledges capsize, or remain hanging over an abyss, while the puller tumbles down. Then comes the order "lie still!" and there he lies a long while, as sledge holder, until the others can come to help him. The sledges must often be pulled at great speed at one part of the crossing, and slowly during another part. . . . Perhaps the sledges have to be entirely unloaded, or else they are balanced across the boat.

August passed, and the better part of September, during which the laborious march went on, sometimes halted by catastrophes, occasionally making quicker progress.

September 4th happened to be Nils Strindberg's birthday. Andrée wrote in his diary:

I awakened him, giving him letters [which had obviously been put in Andrée's keeping before the flight began] from his sweetheart [Anna] and his relations. It was a real pleasure to see how glad he was.

But it was obvious from the slow, tortuous progress of the expedition, during which the wind repeatedly blew them off their intended course, that the chance of reaching Spitsbergen before winter was slight. The weather was getting colder and the icy winds stronger. Still they struggled on.

September 18th, more than two months after the balloon was abandoned, was a wonderful day for Andrée, Strindberg, and Fraenkel, for on that day, to the south, they sighted White Island. It appeared from a distance like a shield of ice, but the travellers knew that there was dry land beneath. On that day they prepared a special dinner, of which Strindberg kept the menu in his log-book. It read:

Wine.

Chocolate with Mellin's food-flour and Albert biscuits and butter.

Gateau aux raisin

Raspberry syrup sauce.

Port wine 1834 Antonio de Ferrar, given by the King

Speech by Andrée for the King with a royal Hurrah!

National Anthem in unison

Biscuits, butter, cheese

Glass of wine.

But the cold bit deeper, and for some reason the men decided not to make the journey to the barren island but to build a snow hut on an ice floe at which they had arrived in their canvas boat after days of paddling. Game had been plentiful. They had shot a walrus, a Polar bear which came swimming towards them, and some seals and ivory gulls. The hut was solidly constructed of packed snow, over which fresh water was poured until it froze, forming compact walls. It even had a vaulted roof, evidence of Strindberg's civil-engineering experience.

Then, one night, when the three travellers were comfortably settled in their winter dwelling, there was a terrible roaring of water, and the floe on which the hut was built broke in half, so that one wall of the hut was suspended over water. It must have been then that the men decided to make the hazardous trip to White Island and seek a permanent winter camp there. And at this point the diary fails us. We have no idea what happened, but Strindberg noted tersely: "Exciting situation." The small pocket diary found on Andrée's body was so badly decayed that only a few words can be made out. But we know from an entry in Strindberg's almanac that on October 5th he wrote "moved to shore," on the 6th "snowstorm, reconnoitering," and on the 7th "moving." We know that Andrée and his comrades were alive at least until October 17th (which was a Saturday), for Strindberg's almanac contains the words "home 7.5. o'clock a.m." And, as Nils Strindberg was the first to die, the other two must have been alive on that date.

What happened during those last three weeks is a mystery. There is no written record, and the contents of the camp do not tell us very much, though a skilful archaeologist, had he been able to visit the site when the *Bratvaag* landed its crew there in 1930, might have picked up a few clues. There are so many unanswered questions. How soon after Strindberg's burial did the other two die? Why was it that, although the heavy pelts of two Polar bears lay in the camp, they had not been used to floor the tent? Why was no sign of a fireplace found, although there was plenty of driftwood and a good supply of matches? Why hadn't the sleeping bag, which lay between the bodies of Andrée and Fraenkel, been occupied that night? And since there was an abundance of food (the carcass of a shot Polar bear lay in the boat), the two survivors could not have died of starvation. What, then, did they die of? The skeletons provided no evidence.

The death of their friend Strindberg, from what cause

we cannot positively know, must have depressed them. In Andrée's clothing was found a silver bear on a chain which Strindberg always wore round his neck, perhaps a keepsake from his fiancée. Andrée had also kept a golden locket containing a portrait of Anna, no doubt intending to hand this to her, with Strindberg's other belongings, when he returned to Sweden. She must have been a young girl when Strindberg wrote those letters to her, of which several survive besides the one from the balloon quoted in this book. When she finally received them thirty-three years later, she was a woman of middle age.

The skipper of the *Bratvaag* was scornful of the clothing worn by the aeronauts when they were found. There were leather jackets, woollen jerseys, Lapp boots, and substantial stockings, but even these, he thought, were ridiculous garments for an Arctic winter. "I think," he said, "that it was the cold which finished them off," and most people accept his view.

But not all, for we know now that the liver of the Polar bear can be poisonous, and that for this reason the Eskimos never eat it. This fact was not known in Andrée's time. We know that Andrée and his companions lived, to a large extent, on Polar-bear meat, and their deaths may have been due to cumulative poisoning. No one knows for certain. But, if cold and exposure were the causes, it seems ironical that Salomon Andrée, who had made such meticulous preparations for the voyage of the *Eagle*—even providing sledges, provisions, and a boat to help the adventurers' return should the balloon meet with misfortune—should have failed to provide clothing of adequate insulating power to withstand a winter on the ice.

One must also consider the intangible, psychological factor which people call "morale" or "the will to live." The three men, to judge from the diaries, were in good spirits. And yet, when a comrade died, and the two survivors returned, after burying him, to their improvised tent, with the whole Arctic winter ahead of them, it seems possible that, exhausted, dispirited, and ill, they lay down to sleep—and never woke up.

Epilogue

The tragic failure of Andrée to reach the North Pole, and the discovery of his camp a generation afterwards, seem an appropriate point at which to end this book. Long before 1930 the airship and the aeroplane had rendered the free balloon out of date as a serious means of transport. After 1900 even the showmen-aeronauts gradually went out of business; the pleasure-loving crowds which had thronged Vauxhall and Cremorne Gardens had become bored with ballooning and were finding other sources of entertainment, such as the cinema. And the dirigible, or powered airship, though it developed from the free balloon, belongs to a separate chapter in aeronautical history.

However, the free balloon did not altogether die with the coming of the airship and the aeroplane; nor is it dead yet. Around the turn of the century it entered a new golden age as the plaything of wealthy sports men (and women) who were attracted by the very freedom which made it impracticable as a mundane form of transport. By comparison how limited was the airship, forced to cruise at a low altitude under the control of noisy petrol engines, or the even more blatant aeroplane, which

191

thrust brutally through the air, drowning every natural sound in the thunder and vibration of its engines!

Many found the silence and wayward freedom of the balloon much more fascinating than the airship or the aeroplane. The period between 1900 and the outbreak of the First World War in 1914 particularly favoured ballooning as a sport of the rich and well-to-do. First, there were fewer natural hazards and inconveniences than in the pioneer days, and fewer man-made hazards than exist today. One could inflate a balloon in practically any town, since gas was almost universally available. Second, railways had been so developed that one could pack and transport a deflated balloon practically anywhere in Europe and return to one's base with equal ease. Nor were there suspicious and superstitious peasants to deal with when one landed, or large airfields with wide approach lanes from which unauthorized aircraft were barred. So, from the beginning of the twentieth century up to about 1930 (apart from 1914–18), ballooning blossomed as a sport. There were balloon societies, such as the Royal Aero Club, balloon races, such as the famous James Gordon Bennett race, and balloon competitions.

James Gordon Bennett was an American enthusiast who also founded a motor-racing trophy. His aeronautical trophy was intended to encourage the development of powered balloons, or, as he called them, "motor aerostats," but the contest developed into a long-distance race for free balloons, each race taking place in the country of the preceding year's winner. The winner of the first race, in 1906, was an American, Frank P. Lahn, whose balloon the *United States*, having started from Paris, landed at Fylingdales, Yorkshire.

Some remarkable flights were made during this halcyon period. For instance, the Aero Club de France produced some skilful and daring amateur balloonists who took part in races, the prize going to the aeronaut who had covered the greatest distance. In 1899 the Comte de la Vaulx flew from Paris to Korosticheff, near Kiev in Russia, a distance of 1,193 miles, in 35 hours and 40 minutes. Then there were the flights of the involuntary record-breakers who became the prey of the winds. Of these, perhaps the most remarkable flight was that made by a Belgian named Goossens, who was unfortunate enough to make his ascent from Berlin at a time when a fierce storm was raging in the upper atmosphere, with winds of hurricane velocity.

The flight began on September 13th, 1903, and the direction at first was over Holland. There Goossens struck a cyclone which whirled him across Europe at an average speed of ninety miles per hour. First it flung him across Belgium and northern France, where, fearing that he might be blown into the sea, he attempted a landing, but failed. He threw out ballast and the big balloon ascended again. A southerly wind blew it as far as the island of Jersey, after which the wind veered and Goossens found himself driven up the English Channel at a speed which, from his instruments, he calculated as 125 miles per hour. Once again he made a desperate attempt to land, and by a lucky chance he managed to hit the ground at Fretham, near the English coast. He and his companion, an unnamed German, escaped with a severe shaking. Afterwards they estimated that their journey had taken them over 1,400 miles, mostly at speeds approaching 100 miles per hour.

When the First World War began, all free ballooning

ceased in Europe, but captive balloons were used for observation and artillery spotting on several fronts. The sport was renewed when the war ended, and the Gordon Bennett races continued until 1938.

Balloon races on this highly organized international scale ceased with the outbreak of the Second World War and have not been renewed, nor are they likely to be, for today the hazards are too numerous and too great: traffic-crowded air corridors, overhead power lines, and —in Europe, at least—a more tightly controlled, regimented form of life, in which the free balloon can have no place. Yet there are still balloon enthusiasts, both in Europe and in the United States, and individual flights continue to be made.

Since the First World War the balloon, both manned and unmanned, has entered a new phase of development. With the invention of new and improved materials for the envelope much greater heights have been reached, and balloons carrying measuring instruments have been increasingly used by military and civil authorities for weather observation and space research. But manned flight also continues. Some daring aeronauts have reached heights far greater than that attained by James Glaisher. One such man was Captain Hawthorne C. Grey, who established a record of 42,470 feet in 1927. He was found dead on the floor of his open gondola when the balloon came down, but the height was recorded on a barograph.

Experiments were then made with closed gondolas. In 1931 the Swiss Auguste Piccard and Paul Kipfer rose to 51,793 feet, and in a later ascent to 55,577 feet. This record was subsequently beaten several times: in 1933 by an American, Major C. L. Fordney, who ascended

to 61,237 feet, and in 1935 when the American balloon
Explorer III, flown by Captain Albert W. Stevens and
Captain Orvil A. Anderson, rose to 72,395 feet—nearly
fourteen miles above the earth's surface.

Plastic stratospheric balloons came into use after the
Second World War, the first of which, an unmanned
aerostat called *Skyhook*, reached an altitude of 100,000
feet on September 25th, 1957. A balloon called *Man High*,
with its pilot, Lieutenant Colonel David G. Simons,
enclosed in an atmospherically sealed capsule, rose
to over 102,000 feet in 1959, the highest altitude ever
reached by a manned balloon. It was a magnificent feat
of human endurance, since at that time the physical and
chemical reactions of the human body at such enormous
altitudes—let alone emotional stress and mental disturb-
ance—were not known with certainty. Lieutenant Colonel Simons deserves to stand beside the greatest of the
aeronauts.

Turning from high-altitude to long-distance flights,
in December 1958 four British enthusiasts, Colin Mudie
and his wife Rosemary, and "Bushy" Eiloart and his son
Tim, made a gallant attempt to fly the Atlantic. Their
balloon, called the *Small World*, had many unusual features. It was made of polyethylene, and the car it supported was constructed as a small boat, so that, if the
aeronauts were forced down, they could continue their
journey by sea. The boat-car was equipped with radio
and a number of scientific instruments, and a great deal
of research was put into the project, including extensive
pre-flight testing. Each member of the crew had his or
her particular function. Colin Mudie was designer of the
balloon and the boat, Rosemary Mudie was photographer
and in charge of food supplies, Tim Eiloart was radio

operator and meteorologist, and "Bushy" Eiloart was captain and pilot of the balloon.

After setting out from Tenerife in the Canary Islands they had an eventful flight of 1,200 miles. They used a guide rope as Green had done in the *Nassau* over a century before, but were so troubled by storms and thermals (uprising currents of air) that they frequently lost gas when the balloon was forced upwards, and at other times had to throw out ballast when storms threatened to force them down into the sea. It was almost impossible to maintain a constant altitude, as they had hoped to do. Eventually the balloon came down for the last time; after cutting away the boat-car by quick-release mechanism they made the rest of the journey in their tiny sail-boat—over 1,500 miles—until they reached Barbados. So the Atlantic still remains unconquered by the free balloon.

The man-carrying balloon is now nearly two hundred years old. Though it seems certain that the balloon will continue to be employed for meteorological observation, its use as a means of human transport is over, save for the few adventurous spirits who, in the words of Shakespeare, still wish to ride "upon the bosom of the air."

Index

197

Index

Index